THE SOCIAL TRIUMPH
OF THE ANCIENT CHURCH

THE SOCIAL TRIUMPH
OF THE ANCIENT CHURCH

by

Shirley Jackson Case

BOOKS FOR LIBRARIES PRESS
FREEPORT, NEW YORK

First Published 1933
Reprinted 1971

BR
163
C3
1971

INTERNATIONAL STANDARD BOOK NUMBER:
0-8369-5880-2

LIBRARY OF CONGRESS CATALOG CARD NUMBER:
76-164596

PRINTED IN THE UNITED STATES OF AMERICA

CONTENTS

PREFACE

THE CHAPTERS OF THIS BOOK WERE DELIVERED, IN A SOME-
what abbreviated form, as the Rauschenbusch Memo-
rial Lectures at Colgate-Rochester Divinity School during Alumni Week, April 18-21, 1933. Twenty years ago
when on a brief lecture visit at Rochester Theological
Seminary I first made the acquaintance of the late Professor Rauschenbusch. His kindliness on that occasion
and his sympathetic reception of a younger man's message still remain a vivid and inspiring memory. It
affords me genuine satisfaction to have the privilege of
bearing testimony to my esteem for Professor Rauschenbusch and his work.

The lecturer wishes to avail himself of this opportunity to express his gratitude to the president, the other
members of the faculty, and the alumni and friends of
Colgate-Rochester Divinity School, whose generous hospitality toward the lecturer and his message will be long
and gratefully remembered.

SHIRLEY JACKSON CASE

University of Chicago

I. *Ancient Religion and Human Values*

I

Ancient Religion and Human Values

IN THE WORLD WHERE CHRISTIANITY AROSE IT WAS COM-
monly believed that human welfare was the business of
Deity. Mankind had not been charged with the task of
effecting its own social salvation. The highest values
available for the individual and the group were generally assumed to be the gifts of heaven. This conviction was shared alike by Jews and by Gentiles.

The Jews ardently adhered to a theocratic social
ideal. The sufferings endured by their ancestors
throughout the tempestuous course of their history had
in no wise shaken their confidence in God as the preserver and savior of his people. The manner of this
divine assistance might be portrayed in varying imagery, according to the views of the several interpreters
who ventured to define God's procedure, but all were
agreed that ideal conditions of life could be brought to
realization, and enduringly established, only by the
action and power of Deity himself. In the meantime
the pious man recognized his obligation to serve his
fellows, yet even in this effort his standard of conduct
was God-given. Devotion to the welfare of humanity,
whether in the home, the community, or the state, was
inseparable from one's duty to Jehovah. To love God
and do his will was the primary and fundamental com-
mandment.

3

The Jews who preached Christianity in the earliest years of its history perpetuated the same type of thinking. Human efforts, in and of themselves, would never insure the highest social values. These could not be attained until that future moment when God would establish immediately, or by the aid of his properly authenticated representative in the person of the Anointed One, a new order of existence in fulfillment of the pledge given in days of old to Abraham and his descendants. Even in its noblest manifestation, the practice of good-will by men was but an imperfect image of God's good pleasure.

The gentiles, in their own way, were no less devoted than the Jews to the notion of a divinely established society. The gods were the authors and sustainers of civilization. They had intervened to bring order out of chaos at the very dawn of history. Under their tutelage men had learned to till the soil, to build cities, to establish civic and national governments, to fare forth upon the sea with their wares, and to cultivate the various arts. Even in the efficiently administered Roman Empire divine powers were thought to be everywhere present and active beneficently or banefully in the daily experiences of mankind. Prosperity was a token of the gods' favor, while calamity was a sure sign of their displeasure. Abundant crops, successful business, bodily health, good government, favorable meteorological conditions, freedom from pestilences and earthquakes, and all that went to make society safe and happy, were assumed by the great masses of people in the Roman

4

world to be a direct result of heaven's favor—or at least an evidence that the anger of the divinities had not been incurred. On the other hand, every form of personal or social misfortune was ascribed to the action of unfriendly supernatural forces.

I

The disciples of Epicurus were the only persons who denied outright the validity of this popular opinion. They boldly alleged that the social order, whether good or bad, was entirely a natural and human phenomenon with which no divinity, either friendly or hostile, had the slightest concern. Man had brought upon himself needless anxieties by falsely supposing that supernatural beings interfered in mundane affairs. Epicurean teachers admonished society to shake off this intolerable burden of error. Since traditional religion seemed to them to be man's worst enemy, they extravagantly lauded the founder of their school for the benefits he had bestowed upon the human race by opening up a way of escape. It was he who had defiantly raised his head against a superstition that kept human life lying "foully prostrate upon earth, pressed down under the weight of religion."

Preachers of the Epicurean gospel continued for centuries to be relentless critics of the supernaturalistic social philosophy current in the gentile world. They never wearied of protesting against its baneful influence; it was a lowering storm cloud with no silver lining. It had been responsible for inventing meddlesome deities who filled mankind with shuddering awe, and it had resulted in a wasteful expenditure of strength and substance upon the building of temples and the observance of multitudinous religious ceremonies throughout the whole known world. Mortals had brought upon themselves dire distress by "handing over all things to the gods and supposing all things to be guided by their nod." Thus society had become god-ridden by the folly of men. "What groans did they beget for themselves, what wounds for us, what tears for our children!" exclaims Lucretius in an eloquent moment.[1]

The Epicureans were not blind to other defects in the social order. It was essential to their philosophical system that everything in the world should be so used as to contribute in the largest possible degree to human happiness. They not only rejected religion, but condemned every form of activity that involved distress for mankind. They protested against the current lust for worldly goods, not on the ground that wealth was in itself evil, but because in the end it brought unhappiness to its possessor. Similarly they discounted the value of high position in society. Up to a certain point, irresistible power and much property might yield satisfaction and a sense of security in human affairs, but happiness depended ultimately upon the tranquillity of one's soul and its freedom from insatiable ambition. They lauded the ideal of fellowship in all human relations and affirmed that, of all the things which wisdom

[1] See Lucretius, *Nature of Things*, I. 62-79; V. 1194-1240.

6

provides for the happiness of the whole life, by far the most important is the acquisition of friends. Those persons with whom friendly relations could not be established should be avoided. Above all, one should strive to make no enemies.

While the disciples of Epicurus were only a minority in the population of the Roman Empire during the first and second centuries of the Christian Era, they did represent some of the most vigorous thinkers and influential persons in the society of the time. One regrets that they did not put forward a more constructive program for effecting social ameliorations. They certainly felt a keen urge to deliver their neighbors from the troubles by which they were so universally afflicted, but the proposed way of release offered a wholly inadequate solution of the tremendous problems involved. It aimed only at the salvation of the individual, not at the healthful reconstitution of the life of the group. As the Epicureans were atomists in physics, so they were individualists in their interpretation of human relations. Mankind's condition was to be improved simply by making converts to the Epicurean philosophy. This ideal meant virtually the renunciation of society as at present organized, except for membership in the Epicurean brotherhood. To participate actively in the existing social order, and, if need be, to spend one's self utterly for the common good, was a possibility that seems never to have come within the Epicurean range of vision.

A more widely influential movement among the in-

7

telligentsia of the Roman Empire was the Stoic propaganda. By the beginning of the Christian Era it had become deeply concerned with the problems of society and had drawn followers from all classes of the population. It gave inspiration and comfort to the wealthy Seneca, the poor slave Epictetus, and the imperial ruler Marcus Aurelius. In so far as it was possible for any "philosophy" to become a possession of the common man, Stoicism may be said to have enjoyed that distinction in the Roman world of early Christian times.

The Stoic rejection of the traditional religions was less drastic than that of the Epicureans, but toward the popular belief that the specific blessings and accidents of life were conditioned by the will of freakish gods its attitude was emphatically negative. The Stoic aspired to be "religious" without being "superstitious."[2] His deity was the primal divine reason that now pervaded all men and things. The world was thus dominated by an all-wise providence, active in all its parts, whose will was only good. The sole source of evil was man's failure to live in accordance with the possibilities of his best self. But even the wicked deeds of men are ultimately subject to an ever-ruling providence for good. In the words of Cleanthes' famous hymn to Zeus: "Nothing that happens upon earth is wrought apart from thee, O Deity, whether through the divine ethereal region or in the sea, except such evil deeds as men do in their own folly. But thou knowest how to

[2] Marcus Aurelius would have posterity remember him as one who was θεοσεβὴς χωρὶς δεισιδαιμονίας (Meditations, V. 31, 14).

8

right even their excesses and to bring order out of disorder and things unlovely are made lovely with thee. For thou hast so joined all things together, the good with the evil, that there is over all one eternal reason which they who are wicked among mortals shun and push aside. Ill-starred, they ever yearn to possess good things, and neither perceive nor heed the universal law of God. If only they would obey it with understanding they would have a happy life."[3]

The great Stoic teachers were keenly aware of many vicious features in the life of their day and gave themselves devotedly, according to their lights, to the task of bringing about an improvement in the unhappy state of affairs. By diligence in preaching they won many converts to their way of thinking. Also, they were ever ready to draw the practical inferences involved in their fundamental teaching that the Deity is the father of all men, and therefore all human beings are equal by divine right. They demanded that everyone in authority discharge the duties of office for the common good. They condemned outright those class distinctions that artificially separated society into different strata; in the sight of God the slave was as estimable as the monarch. They were ardent advocates of the republican form of government, as against the monarchical, and they vigorously protested against warfare between men and nations. Racial and national rivalries were utterly

[3] Lines 11 ff., in von Arnim, *Stoicorum veterum fragmenta,* I, 122. See also Marcus Aurelius, *Meditations,* V. 44; VI. 36; VII. 75; IX. 28.

9

repudiated in favor of the gospel of universal brotherhood. Justice, mercy, friendship, and all the good things of the world, being essentially the gifts of heaven, all men as sons of Deity were alike entitled to share.

Among the preachers of charity in Roman society, Stoics were, as a matter of course, the most outspoken. They were also the most severe critics of promiscuous beneficence, whether practised for the sake of show, or as a mere habitual concession to the customs of the time. Selfish motives in conduct, whether for convenience or for glory, were anathema to them, even when exercised on behalf of one's unfortunate neighbor. The Stoic even went so far as to condemn charity if it rested upon no more rational basis than that of the mere feeling of pity.[4] Throwing pennies to beggars, by one who refused to recognize that the beggar had the same divine parentage and was worthy of the same respect as the richest philanthropist in the Empire, was a procedure that could not be tolerated. The beggar himself also came in for a word of criticism. Often his greatest need, so he was told, was not money or bread, but an increased self-respect that would enable him to look upon the accidents of the social order with a greater measure of equanimity and a stouter determination to be unmoved by misfortune. Poverty, like sickness, does not necessarily involve unhappiness, if the mind is not impoverished and diseased. The Stoic advocated as vigorously as did Paul, though on

[4] Note particularly Seneca, *Clemency*, II. 5.

different grounds, the desirability of learning to be content irrespective of one's physical status.[5]

Not unnaturally, critics of the Stoics often charged them with being hard-hearted and ungenerous; their humanitarianism seemed to be too doctrinaire. As a matter of fact, adherents of this school were rarely in a position to practice benevolence on any large scale, since many of their most distinguished representatives were but scantily equipped with worldly goods. Yet there were men of wealth, like Seneca, who squarely faced economic and philanthropic problems. To acquire wealth by unfair means could have no justification in the opinion of Seneca, but the possession of property justly acquired was not inconsistent with the pursuit of philosophy. Seneca refused to call riches a good thing; for, said he, if they were such they would make all of their holders good; but since they are often found in the possession of bad men, they cannot in and of themselves be termed good. Nevertheless, they were desirable and useful, and capable of contributing much comfort to a man's life. In fact, the wise man should welcome the opportunities that were made possible to him through the possession of wealth. It opened up to him a wide field for the exhibition of temperance and

[5] "Virtue alone insures a blessed life. . . . A wise man is touched by sorrow but not overcome by it. . . . He will exhibit virtue in wealth if he is permitted to possess it, but if not, in poverty; or in his native country if it shall be possible, if not, in exile; as a general if he can, if not, as a soldier; in health if he can, if not, in weakness. Whatever fortune comes to him, he will effect something memorable from it. . . . Pain, poverty, ignominy, imprisonment, exile, and whatever dreadful things come upon him, they are tamed by him."—*Epistles,* LXXXV. 40 f.

generosity in social relations. Riches were masters in the house of the foolish, but valuable servants in the house of the true philosopher.

Riches involved their possessor in serious responsibilities. If he were a wise man be would be guided by the same honest purpose in the disposition of his wealth that had dominated his efforts in its attainment. The duty of expending one's means was, according to the Stoics, to be taken very seriously. Seneca assured his readers that if they supposed this to be an easy matter they were entirely wrong. The rational man must see to it that his bounty is not distributed on momentary impulse or at random. Great care had to be taken in choosing the objects of benevolence. Above all, it was important that the philanthropist should not create, either in himself or in the recipient of his charity, a loss of respect for the inherent dignity of the human personality. While charity should be distributed with discrimination, it must not be restricted to any special class of person; the philanthropist owes a duty to the whole of mankind. It matters not to him whether the person in need is free-born, freedman, or slave, whether he is a member of one's own household or a stranger from foreign parts; wherever there is a needy human being, there is a proper place for the display of beneficence.

When in the Stoic scheme of thinking the divine will had been made wholly good, and the responsibility for the conduct of human affairs had been placed squarely upon the shoulders of men made in the image

12

of the Deity, one might expect to find the emergence of a very active interest in bringing about, through concrete human efforts, a higher realization of practical social values. But here again we meet disappointment. The Stoic, like the Epicurean, was essentially an individualist. His belief in divine providence issued in a virtual fatalism. Toward his environment, whether it was good or bad, the wise man would assume an attitude of passive submission and strive to suppress all desires. He would be unmoved by either success or misfortune. Thus social ills were to be alleviated by cultivating individual serenity of spirit. God in his wisdom allowed evil to exist—it was indeed inherent in a world of natural relations—and it was no task of one who was loyal to the Deity to attempt to alter God's world. Only by a personal reformation from within, as men were urged to live true to their best selves, could the Stoic preacher hope to effect social betterment. Not until all citizens had become wise men of the Stoic type could the evils of society be abolished. In the meantime one preached the Stoic social virtues that ought to be practiced by everyone who would live wisely in the sight of God and men; but active participation in social tasks, though necessary under certain circumstances, was a hindrance rather than an aid to the attainment of the Stoic ideal.

Notwithstanding the noble sentiments and the sincere humanitarian attitude of Stoicism, its temper was too individualistic to result in any systematic organization of a definite program for social ameliorations.

13

Even an emperor, with all the magnificent opportunities for social reform that lay in his power, prized above everything else those moments of leisure for self-analysis and meditation that could be snatched from busy days in discharging the duties of his imperial office.[6]

[6] The fatalism and individualism of Marcus Aurelius are well illustrated in such sentiments as the following:

"The duration of human life is a mere point in time, its being is fleeting, it is dimly perceived, the composition of the entire body readily putrefies, and the soul is a spinning-top, and fortune is hard to determine, and fame is uncertain. In a word, all things that have to do with the body are like a river, and all things that have to do with the soul are like a dream and smoke; life is a combat and the sojourn of a foreigner, and posthumous fame is oblivion. What is it, then, that is able to furnish guidance? One thing, and one only, philosophy. And this means to preserve one's inner divinity immune from insult and harm, master of pleasures and pains, doing nothing aimlessly or deceitfully and pretentiously, not in need of another's doing or not doing anything; and, furthermore, accepting what happens by chance or necessity as coming from the source whence one's divinity came; but, above all, awaiting death with a genial disposition, as nothing but a dissolution of the elements of which each living thing is composed. And if no harm ever comes to the elements themselves in the perpetual change of each thing into another, why should anyone view with suspicion the change and complete dissolution of all things? For it is in accordance with nature, and nothing that is in accordance with nature is evil" (*Meditations*, II. 17). Speaking of the unideal conditions of life in the society of the time, the emperor expresses himself thus: "Affairs are, in a way, so obscure to not a few philosophers—not dilettantes either—that they seem to be entirely incomprehensible. Indeed, even to the Stoics themselves they seem hard to comprehend. . . . In such gloom and clutter, and in such a flow of being and time, both of motion and of things in motion, I do not even perceive what there is that is capable of being highly desired or whole-heartedly pursued. On the contrary, it is necessary to control one's self and await the natural dissolution, and not to be distressed at the delay but to acquiesce in the following opinions: first, that nothing will overtake me that is not in accordance with the nature of all things; and, second, that it is possible for me never to act contrary to my god and divinity. For there is no one who compels me to transgress against this inward monitor" (*Ibid.*, V. 10).

Yet one should note that Marcus Aurelius, on returning to Rome after

II

It would be altogether unfair to the memory of the ancient philosophers, and other public-spirited individuals in the Roman Empire, to leave the impression that they were devoid of sympathy for the poor and unfortunate or were lacking in generous activities. The charitable impulses of the Gentiles have not always been appreciated by students interested to show by contrast the superior quality of Christianity's humanitarian motives and actions. While it is entirely apparent that Christianity introduced a new and much more fruitful spirit of compassion than had previously obtained in ancient society, this new attitude was not so original as has sometimes been assumed; and one must also recognize that the Christian movement, in its social practices and theories, perpetuated many of the weaknesses previously current in its heathen environment.[7]

an absence of eight years, gave out 200 denarii apiece to the people, this being the largest donation ever received at any one time. He also canceled all debts to the imperial and public treasury covering a period of forty-six years, and gave money to many cities that had suffered from earthquakes. Dio Cassius, 72.32.

[7] The subject has called forth an extensive literature. E. Chastel, *Études historiques sur l'influence de la charité durant les premiers siècles chrétiens* (Paris, 1853); A. Monnier, *Histoire de l'assistance publique dans les temps anciens et modernes* (Paris, 1857); A. Tollemer, *Des origines de la charité catholique ou de l'état de la misère et de l'assistance chez les chrétiens pendant les premiers siècles de l'Église* (Paris, 1863); M. Magetti, *La genesi e l'evoluzione della beneficenza* (Ravenna, 1890); G. Uhlhorn, *Geschichte der christlichen Liebestätigkeit*, 2. Aufl., 3 vols. (Stuttgart, 1895), of which the first volume of the first edition appeared in English, *Christian Charity in the Ancient Church* (Edinburgh, 1883); L. Lallemand, *Histoire de la charité*, 4 (5) vols. (Paris, 1902-12); W. Liese, *Geschichte der*

A benevolent attitude toward the unfortunate, the poor, and the outcasts, whose number was legion in the Roman Empire, manifested itself in a wide variety of ways. When expressed by government officials, frequently the main purpose of charity was to preserve political stability and maintain respect for the ruling class. When voluntarily practiced by individuals, undoubtedly generosity was often inspired by selfish motives. It gave one social prestige to be known as a person about whom clients swarmed, or a sponsor of expensive shows for the enjoyment of the populace, or a donor of magnificent buildings to augment the glory of a city. These were features played up in the headlines on the front page of the daily newspaper, so to speak, but they are not a just criterion by which to measure the beneficent temper of the ancient world, as they are similarly inadequate to measure the depth and sincerity of the beneficent spirit in the twentieth century. Lust for praise or posthumous fame could display itself then as now, but it must not be allowed to obscure those deeper currents of human sympathy and finer appreciation of human values that were to be found in Roman society even beyond the circles of Christian influence.

Caritas, 2 vols. (Freiburg i. Br., 1922); article "Charité" in F. Cabrol and H. Leclercq, *Dictionnaire d'archéologie chrétienne et de liturgie,* Vol. III, cols. 598-653 (Paris, 1913); article "Liberalitas" in Pauly-Wissowa, *Real-Encyclopädie der classischen Allertumswissenschaft,* Vol. XIII, 1 (25. Halbband), cols. 82-93 (Stuttgart, 1926); S. J. Case (editor), *A Bibliographical Guide to the History of Christianity* (Chicago, 1931), items 287-294.

16

The beneficent activities characteristic of ancient society were most conspicuously exemplified in the case of various government officials. Augustus, the first emperor, was long remembered as the model benefactor of humanity. With a candor that is, perhaps, not unbecoming in an imperial prince, he listed a long series of favors gratuitously showered upon his subjects.[8] At the very beginning of his administration he complied with the instructions of Julius Cæsar's will, which granted to every Roman plebeian three hundred sesterces.[9] On his own initiative, when he was consul for the fifth time, Augustus made a similar gift of four hundred sesterces per person from the spoils of war. In his tenth consulship he repeated this donation, and in his eleventh he purchased at his own expense on three different occasions grain for free distribution. At three different times during the twelfth year that he was tribune he again dispersed four hundred sesterces. He says that on each of these occasions the allotment was made to not less than 250,000 persons. Later he gave sixty denarii apiece to the 320,000 plebs in Rome. When he was consul for the fifth time he distributed to each man in the colonies of his soldiers a thousand sesterces, about 120,000 persons sharing in the donation. Also, in his thirteenth consulship he gave, in addition to free grain, an allotment of sixty denarii to the plebs

[8] *Deeds of Augustus,* Chaps. 15-24.

[9] The sestertius was a small silver coin equivalent to about four and one-third U. S. cents, and four sestertii made one denarius, about seventeen cents. But the purchasing power of the cent would have been much greater in the ancient world than it is today.

17

in number more than 200,000. These various gifts in money totaled the equivalent of upward of thirty million dollars.

Additional sums in large amounts were also made available by Augustus for the purchase of real estate. On different occasions he bought from municipalities land which he gave to the soldiers. For Italian farms he expended about six hundred million sesterces, and for land in the provinces about two hundred and sixty million. Also to the soldiers who received farms at the expiration of their service he distributed gratuities in money to the amount of four hundred million sesterces. On four occasions he aided the public treasury from his private means to the extent of one hundred and fifty million sesterces, and to the military treasury established on his advice he donated one hundred and seventy million sesterces as an endowment to yield gratuities for soldiers who had served twenty years or more in the army. Again, when the supply of grain ran low he came to the rescue, sometimes providing for the needs of 400,000 men and sometimes for more, appropriating for this purpose the income from his own land and property.

Augustus' expenditure upon public enterprises alone involved a vast outlay. He restored almost a hundred temples that were falling into decay, or constructed new ones. He erected theaters and aqueducts, he provided funds for the building of roads and bridges, and he reared or adorned many public buildings. At times he remitted the gifts made to him by municipalities and

18

colonies on the occasion of his various triumphs. Still another form of his generosity, greatly appreciated by the populace, consisted in his expenditures upon public entertainments. He recounts eight occasions when he had given gladiatorial exhibitions participated in by about ten thousand contestants. Five times he sponsored athletic games, gathering for the purpose performers from all quarters of the world. The expenses of the lesser games, ordinarily given by the magistrates, were assumed by him at different times. On twenty-six occasions he presented hunts of African wild beasts in the circus, the forum, and the amphitheaters, at which approximately thirty-five hundred animals had been killed. Once he made possible for the people the spectacle of a naval battle, for which he excavated and constructed an artificial lake capable of accommodating thirty standard ships and many of smaller size. In this battle three thousand men, in addition to the rowers, participated.

Tiberius was reputed to have been more niggardly in the distribution of his gifts, but the example of Augustus was followed in the main by successive rulers for centuries. Doles of grain, presents of money to the populace, and the staging of spectacles were forms of beneficence that continued to be displayed, not only by emperors, but by other officials, often when the financial situation of the donor was hardly adequate to the task. It was not uncommon for cities that had been visited by earthquakes to be relieved of taxes for a longer or shorter period, frequently money was loaned without interest from the personal funds of an official, poor people were encouraged to raise large families by the aid of the imperial treasury, and a general policy of paternalism with reference to the needy was practiced by the government. If we are to trust Suetonius, even Augustus had been aware of the evil consequences likely to attend these forms of public charity. Augustus is quoted as saying once that he was disposed to abolish forever the practice of distributing grain at the public expense because people tended to become so dependent upon these gifts that they were too lazy to work their farms, but he sought to remedy the evil by other means rather than by withdrawing this type of benefaction.[10]

Examples of private generosity on the part of well-to-do people in Roman society are also numerous. Funds were made available for the endowment of schools, the construction of public buildings, and the celebration of games. In the time of Pliny the Younger an old law still in force prohibited any corporate city from inheriting an estate. But one of Pliny's friends, apparently unaware of this statute, had left a fourth of his property to their native town, Comum. Pliny recognized that this gift was contrary to law, yet he assumed that the ancient legislation might be ignored and that the city might properly receive the 400,000 sesterces left it by the will of the donor. This was the same town to which Pliny gave over a million sesterces to establish and endow a library, and another half-

[10] Suetonius, *Augustus*, 42.

million for the support of the children of poor but worthy parents, and pledged one-third of the amount necessary to maintain a local school. In another instance reported by Pliny a wealthy man of Pontus, who apparently was aware of the existence of the old law, had left all of his estate to Pliny but had made a personal request that he keep 50,000 sesterces for himself and hand over the remainder to the cities of Heraclea and Tios. The money was to be used either for public buildings or for the celebration of games.[11]

A widespread type of benefaction participated in not alone by officials of the government, but also by private donors, was the establishment of foundations known as *alimenta*. These were designed to provide for the support and education of children whom poor parents could not maintain and who otherwise might have been sold into slavery or allowed to perish by exposure. Property was given to municipalities, or sums were set aside by imperial authority, to purchase food for indigent boys and girls even while they remained under the parental roof. Nerva had authorized the establishment of corporations for this purpose and from that day onward both emperors and private individuals were conspicuous in these charities, until the decay of the Empire's prosperity brought them to an end and resulted in the disappearance of older endowments.

The alimentary tables that have been discovered re-

[11] Pliny, *Epistles,* I. 8; IV. 13; V. 7; VII. 18; X. 79 f. See further, S. Dill, *Roman Society from Nero to Marcus Aurelius* (New York, 1904), pp. 190-195; 223-230.

21

veal the extensive operation of this form of social service. One learns, for example, that Trajan gave the town of Veleia the annual income from 1,044,000 sesterces invested at five per cent as a fund to support boys up to the age of eighteen and girls until fourteen. The name of Faustina, the wife of Antoninus Pius, was given to girls who were supported from her generosity. A kind-hearted lady, Caelia Macrina, established a fund in perpetuity to feed one hundred children, boys and girls, between the ages of six and thirteen years. A certain donor provided drugs and other remedies for free distribution among the poor in his native town. Illustrations of these types of charity might be almost indefinitely multiplied. Whatever may be said of other forms of benefaction, at least in this instance it must be conceded that there was a large humanitarian element involved, even though it be granted that emperors were primarily interested to preserve intact the declining population.[12]

Another form of social activity often associated with the idea of charity is met with in the various guilds in the Roman Empire, the *collegia,* as they were called. Their establishment was popularly credited to Numa and lauded as one of the most admirable enactments of that idealized ancient monarch. By this means he had, it was said, eliminated the vicious rivalries of older parties and focused interest upon the principal

[12] For details, particularly the inscriptions referring to these activities, see the article "Alimenta" in Pauly-Wissowa, *Real-Encyclopädie der classischen Altertumswissenschaft,* Vol. I (Stuttgart, 1894), cols. 1484-1489.

22

occupations of daily life. The common people had been grouped according to eight principal arts or trades, as follows: musicians, goldsmiths, builders, dyers, shoemakers, tanners, workers in brass, and potters. Other persons who could not be fitted into any one of these classifications were organized into a separate corporation with a promiscuous membership.[13] In imperial times these associations had become well-nigh innumerable. They were to be found in all parts of the Mediterranean world and represented a wide variety of social interests. Their existence and activities are abundantly attested by numerous inscriptions.[14]

The measure of service rendered by the *collegia* to needy persons in the Roman world seems, however, to have been slight in comparison with the opportunities that one might imagine to have been within the power of these numerous and widely dispersed associations. They must have touched almost every side of the religious, economic, and social life of the day. There were guilds of every sort of laborer, mechanic, trades-

[13] Plutarch, *Numa*, 17.

[14] Good brief accounts of the *collegia* may be found in S. Dill, *op. cit.*, pp. 254-286; F. F. Abbott, *The Common People of Ancient Rome* (New York, 1917), pp. 205-234; article "Guilds (Greek and Roman)" in Hastings, *Encyclopaedia of Religion and Ethics*, Vol. VI (New York, 1914), pp. 218-221. The most detailed treatment of the subject is by J. P. Waltzing, *Étude historique sur les corporations professionnelles chez les Romains*, 4 vols. (Louvain, 1895-1900). An extensive bibliography is given in Vol. I, pp. 17-30, and Vol. III reproduces the pertinent Greek and Latin inscriptions. See also E. Ziebarth, *Das griechische Vereinswesen* (Leipzig, 1896); F. Poland, *Geschichte des griechischen Vereinswesen* (Leipzig, 1909); M. Radin, *The Legislation of the Greeks and Romans on Corporation* (New York, 1910); and the article "Collegium" in Pauly-Wissowa, *op. cit.*, Vol. IV (Stuttgart, 1901), cols. 380-480.

23

man, property owner, or profession. Rich and poor, freedmen and slaves, and people of different social strata, were sometimes represented in the same group. Whatever may be the kernel of truth in the tradition of their official establishment by Numa, unquestionably the source of their popularity in the imperial age was a spontaneous desire for their existence on the part of the common people. Except in the case of older guilds officially recognized, the authorities looked upon them with suspicion as likely to give to malcontents too much freedom for seditious propaganda. Already in the days of Julius Cæsar and Augustus it had been found necessary to disband many popular associations,[15] and subsequent rulers were distinctly hostile toward proposals for the formation of new *collegia.*[16] Yet the motive forces calling them into being could not be successfully resisted; they answered to an irrepressible demand from within society itself which even the most watchful authorities could not effectively eradicate.

Notwithstanding an indomitable social urge behind the guilds, humanitarian interests and beneficent motives appear to have played only a minor rôle in their aims and activities. Quite incidentally, if at all, did

[15] Suetonius, *Cæsar,* 42; *Augustus,* 32.

[16] For example, Trajan refused to permit the organization of an association of firemen in Nicomedia; and while he could not deny to the confederate Greek city of Amiseni the right to form an *eranos,* he regarded the move with suspicion as likely to result in disturbance to the peace. Pliny, *Epistles,* X. 33 f. (42 f.) and 93 f. Tertullian surmises, and no doubt properly, that this fear was a serious obstacle to the legalization of the Christian societies (*Apology,* xxxviii. 2).

they attempt to improve current conditions of life, and the practice of charity even within the limits of the group was at best only a secondary consideration. Nor were they concerned with constructive efforts to better the economic status of their members, to obtain privileges or monopolies in business, to effect political reforms, to secure a more adequate wage for laborers, or to correct the injustices of slavery. Their main function seems to have been simply to satisfy the individual craving for acquaintance, companionship, and social relaxation among persons engaged in common tasks and callings.

The largest measure of mutual helpfulness realized in the *collegia* was connected with the provision for funerals, an interest that was prominent in many guilds. It was relatively easy for burial societies to secure a legal permit to operate. The society adopted a tutelary deity whose name it bore and under whose protection the members gathered at appointed times and places for meetings or meals that gave a festive character to the assembly in spite of its more somber duties. The guilds not only provided for a decent burial of one otherwise unable to secure this privilege, but they undertook worthily to perpetuate the memory of the deceased. In the main the membership consisted of poor people, often of the slave or freedman class, and it must have been no easy task to maintain a sufficient fund for even their humble needs. This was derived from initiation fees and monthly dues, but

25

sometimes the association elicited the interest of well-to-do patrons who built chapels in which to assemble and furnish money for feasts.

But even funerary guilds were scarcely charitable institutions in any strict sense of that term. One's status in the group depended upon financial ability to pay the initiation fee and meet the monthly dues. The delinquent member forfeited his rights and needy outsiders were granted no favors. The tenor of the numerous inscriptions can hardly be said to reflect a beneficent temper.[17] It is true that a liberated slave might leave an endowment of one thousand sesterces to the rag-dealers guild, of which he was a member, but the gift was to endow an annual banquet to be celebrated at his tomb, where not less than twelve members of the society were to assemble for the ceremony.[18] Or one left a sum the yearly income of which was to be used in celebrating the donor's birthday. These acts were charitable to the

[17] The funerary society at Lanuvium, for example, has left a lengthy record of its rules and procedure. The entrance fee was one hundred sesterces and one amphora of good wine, and the monthly charge was five asses. If a member was six months in arrears at the time of his death he was not entitled to a funeral. But for one whose dues had been properly paid a sum of three hundred sesterces was expended upon his burial. When a slave died, if an unkind master refused to surrender his body, the society conducted an "imaginary funeral" in his honor. But a member who committed suicide was ignored. A slave member who later secured his freedom had to present the society with one amphora of good wine. An appropriate fine was imposed upon a negligent official of the guild, and many specific rules for the conduct of the association were set forth. The complete inscription is given in Waltzing, *Op. cit.,* III. 643-646.

[18] Waltzing, *op. cit.,* III. 502.

26

memory of the deceased, but offered no relief for the distresses of the living. Even the funerary associations seem never to have conceived of their task as that of heightening human values or ministering substantial relief to unfortunate human beings suffering under the inequalities and cruel necessities of an existing social order.

III

Ancient society, while appreciative of the good things of life and conscious of flagrant evils, felt no impulsion to undertake an extensive modification of its own structure. Generous persons, as individuals, did what they could to remedy the situation, but apparently without ever envisaging the possibility of instituting measures for corporate improvement. Social optimism on the human level had not yet been born. The rehabilitation of human values was not to be effected by men themselves working singly and collectively in the here and now. The ideal state of primitive happiness lay in the distant past, while the murky atmosphere of pessimism hung heavily over the present Age of Iron. The revolving cycle of time would bring in again the Age of Gold, but not as a result of improvements realized through the gradual processes of social evolution operating on the terrestrial plane. A mighty cataclysm would one day dissolve the cosmos into its constituent elements from which once more a Golden Age would arise. Yet this, too, would deteriorate, as

27

the cosmic wheel continued to revolve, bringing round again the Age of Iron.[19]

All that a distressed humanity could hope for was temporary relief. But this was not despised. A measure of help from fellow mortals was welcomed, but this was extensively supplemented by resort to supernatural assistance. The lot of mankind was at the disposal of the gods. Despite the protests of Epicurean and Stoic critics, traditional religious institutions continued to be the instrumentalities by which the great masses of the population among all classes of people in the Roman Empire sought to insure protection and betterment in their struggles against the menacing evils of their time. An elaborate and varied technique had long ago been devised for the accomplishment of this beneficent purpose.

The Roman Empire was preëminently a regime of law. While philosophers made a distinction between the law of God—which for the Stoics was also the law of nature—and the legal enactments of men,[20] popular thinking saw in the orderly maintenance of society's life an expression of the divine will. The wisest human legislators had had recourse to a higher source of wisdom. Minos had regularly sought guidance from Zeus,

[19] Seneca, *Natural Questions,* III. 30.7; also article "Ages of the World (Greek and Roman)" in Hastings, *Encyclopaedia of Religion and Ethics,* I. (New York, 1913), 192-200; S. J. Case, *The Millennial Hope* (Chicago, 1918), pp. 1-47, on "Gentile Hopes."

[20] Note particularly in this connection A. Bill, *La morale et la loi* (Paris, 1928).

28

Lycurgus had often consulted the Pythian goddess, the authors of the Twelve Tables of the Romans had promulgated oracular wisdom, and Numa had ruled the people by "religious devices and divine law."[21] While the Gentiles were more ready than Jews and Christians to credit men with a large measure of initiative and responsibility in establishing adequate legislation for the proper ordering of society, ultimately it was of divine origin.

The common man, who concerned himself little if at all with generalities, acted in his concrete situation on the same principle. He strove to avoid disaster, to escape experienced ills, or to insure success, by recourse to a wide variety of means that current religion had placed at his disposal. He consulted the diviner, he ran to the oracles, he trembled at portents, he sought guidance from the astrologer, he repentantly covered himself with sackcloth and ashes, and he resigned himself hopelessly to the decrees of a cruel or indifferent Destiny. A few daring spirits rose to the Epicurean heights of skeptical scorn, while others found refuge in the practice of Stoic apathy, but the average run of mortals in Roman society lived in a state of perpetual anxiety, to be relieved only by the aid of religion. Among the multiplicity of religious ministrations available, two types may be conveniently differentiated for observation in the present connection. One had to do primarily with the well-being of the group, while

[21] Strabo, XVI. 2. 28 f.; Livy, I. 18; III. 34; Tacitus, *Annals,* III. 26 f.

the other ministered more particularly to the personal feelings and inner needs of the individual.[22]

In earlier times a host of divinities had emerged to safeguard the interests of a specific group. There had been gods to protect the family, the clan, the residents of a particular territory, the members of a race or nation, the inhabitants of a city, and persons engaged in one or another occupation. These deities were charged with the task of warding off disaster from their devotees and insuring for them health, prosperity, and happiness. Throughout centuries of history they had rendered memorable service, and many of them were still highly and gratefully revered as helpers and saviors of mankind by multitudes of people in the Roman Empire. These divine protectors of society had changed or enlarged their functions from time to time with changing conditions in the Mediterranean basin, but so far as their sphere of operation was concerned they were still in popular belief the supernatural guardians of the social order. They were the official protectors of its physical, economic, political, and cultural well-being.

When emperors were deified by popular assent, or by decree of the Senate, the act was expressive of the prevailing sentiment that the affairs of state were divinely ordered. Without the inspiration of this sentiment it is quite improbable that emperor worship ever would have prospered in the Roman world. Con-

[22] During the last two decades many books have appeared dealing with the religious situation in the Roman world of early Christian times. For an introduction to this literature see S. J. Case, *Bibliographical Guide to the History of Christianity* (Chicago, 1931), items 425-441.

versely, when the more efficient emperors attempted to undergird the tottering governmental structure, one of their primary concerns was to set the rites of religion in order and thereby strengthen the supernatural resources of the state. Augustus, Decius, Diocletian, Julian, are conspicuous examples. If one doubts that they themselves always believed the reconstitution of religion to be essential to the success of their administrative reforms, one must still recognize that emperors knew this to be the prevailing opinion of their subjects. Probably, too, it was a more deep-seated feeling with the rulers themselves than has always been recognized by their more skeptical modern interpreters. The new political, civic, and economic program instituted by the joint Augusti, Diocletian and Maximian, certainly was capable of yielding direct social benefits, but these were not left to accredit themselves in their own right. The emperors acted, not in the name of humanity, but by the authority of Jupiter and Hercules, whose representatives they believed themselves to be.[23] And in justice to Diocletian, a notorious persecutor of Christianity, it ought to be noted that from his point of view Christian refusal to revere the official gods of the state was the most serious menace to its welfare that could possibly be imagined. Human institutions might be regulated by man's own efforts, but a society dependent for its welfare upon the pleasure

[23] Diocletian took the title of *Jovius*, and Maximian that of *Herculius*, and the emperors were declared to be *a diis geniti et deorum creatores*.

of the deities could not with impunity continue to insult by neglect its divine protectors.

Julian also, apostate though he was in the view of Christians, ought not too readily to be charged with insincerity. He may have been the victim of a false conviction in believing that the favor of the ancient gods was essential to the welfare of the empire. But he had ample precedent for this opinion, and it must be conceded that the god of the Christians, whom Constantine and his successors had called into the service of the state, had not in Julian's day proved an eminently successful guardian of society's well-being. Julian's attempt to introduce the charitable ideals and practices of Christianity into the pagan religions is notable, yet his motive was religious rather than humanitarian. This was the type of conduct that would please the deities —which was the more important consideration in Julian's mind—and thus win their favor for society. Charity was necessary in human relations because "all homeless and impoverished people are dear to Zeus," hence failure in kindly deeds meant disgrace for the gods and neglect to render them the reverence that was their due. Nor could Julian himself properly show kindness to his subjects if they did not first so act as to win the divine favor; "it is unlawful for me to grant respite or show pity to men who are hateful to the immortal gods."[24]

A second type of religion that prospered in imperial times ministered more directly to the personal needs

[24] Julian, *Letter* 49, 431B and 432.

32

of the individual. There were many such cults. Their value to society as a whole was only secondary to the service they rendered needy individuals by providing a sense of divine reinforcement for the inner life, a consciousness of fellowship among members of the religious group, and in many cases an assurance of a blessed life after death when the spirit had passed on to a new state of bliss forever freed from the unavoidable distresses of the present social order. By a voluntary act devotees attached themselves to the divinities and experienced the psychological satisfactions that normally attended this exercise of one's power of will. More or less elaborate rites of initiation, followed by regular participation in the celebrations of a formal ritual, revived and strengthened the emotions. The consciousness of a new fellowship with the Deity, and a sense of community of interest among the worshipers, fortified them to endure with fresh courage the hard experiences of every-day life. Unquestionably, these voluntary religious associations, often referred to in both ancient and modern literature as the "mysteries," answered to a widely felt need in the Mediterranean world during the early centuries of the Christian Era.

Such was the religious background of the heathen society into which the Christian preachers came with their message of divine love and human brotherhood. Paul, who spent many years of his life in launching the new religion among Gentiles, declared that he worked under the compelling power of love. While he summoned men to have faith in Christ and to live in the hope of his return to establish a new order, the fundamental requirement for a Christian was that, above all else, he should be dominated by love.[25] The Christian religion was, indeed, rooted in Judaism, but the Hebrew law could be summed up in the single sentence "Thou shalt love thy neighbor as thyself."[26] This attitude was also to be given concrete expression in conduct. As a matter of course it was to be displayed first in the brotherhood of the religious society, but, whenever occasion permitted, the Christian was to "do good to all men."[27] In the centuries that followed, Christians kept conspicuously in the foreground this humanitarian interest. They not only accepted but further strengthened the current gentile conviction that it was peculiarly the task of religion to safeguard the highest human values.

The Christian position, noble as it was in sentiment, had its practical disadvantages. Human values that lay outside the range of interests which Christians had been accustomed to regard as properly religious were thereby left to care for themselves—if, indeed, they were not dismissed as indifferent or condemned as illegitimate. Gentiles were wont to include a much wider range of social activities within the proper scope of religion's protection. Especially was this true of the official Roman cults that embraced in their concern all the affairs of a well-ordered state. Christianity, on the

[25] I Cor. 13:13.
[26] Gal. 5:14, quoting Lev. 19:18.
[27] Gal. 6:20.

34

other hand, was the type of religion that concentrated attention upon the individual and gathered its adherents into a voluntary association whose primary aim was to establish a spiritual fellowship among believers loyal to the Christians' God. In this respect Christianity resembled more closely the mystery type of religion, and so quite naturally won its way during the first two centuries of its history in the Roman Empire by furnishing more effectively than did the mysteries the satisfactions to which they had endeavored to minister. But traveling by this highway no religion could become the guardian of social welfare for the Roman world as a whole.

Christianity attained its social triumph in the ancient world by gradually changing its course. Not until it learned to abandon, or at least to supplement extensively, its earlier individualism, was it in a position to meet the wider range of demands current in a society long accustomed to seek divine help in the field of economic, political, and cultural life. Unless Christianity could prove itself capable of making human beings healthier, wealthier, happier, wiser, and politically more powerful, it never could be accepted by Roman society as a religion adequate to its need. Christianity's spiritual ideals for the individual and its abounding humanitarianism, noble as they were, were not generally appropriable in that type of social order. A religion that would protect society had to be integrated fully with the varied activities and interests of the people; it could not remain in grand isolation by set-

35

ting up ideals to which only the few could attain and demanding that its adherents live a cloistered life remote from the concerns of the workaday world.

The change of procedure was not brought about quickly, and not without severe struggles, both internal and external. Rigorous Christian idealists, who sensed the trend of events, might vigorously dissent and save their consciences by attaching themselves to small protesting groups, like the Montanists, devoted to the maintenance of the non-worldly attitudes of an earlier day. But this conflict within the Christian ranks was not the most painful feature in the transition. The Christian rejection of the traditional protectors of Roman society caused chief trouble. On the generally accepted view that society's welfare was insured by the deities, it followed as a matter of course that Christians by refusing allegiance to these divinities were suspected of being instrumental in bringing down upon mankind the wrath of heaven. This was a worse crime against society than it would have been for a Christian now and then to have been found guilty of theft, arson, or murder. When Christians claimed, without fear of contradiction, that no specific crimes could be proved against them and that they were the most law-abiding people in a community, they had not yet met the real issue. Their claim might be true, but still did they not refuse loyalty to the gods who were society's supernatural guardians?

Christians refused to worship the official gods. This was an admitted fact. Then how could they effectively

36

refute the charge that they were the occasion for the calamities that were overtaking the social order? Only by becoming themselves the actual saving leaven in the social structure could they reverse popular suspicion. By industry and frugality they must become a stabilizing force in economic life, in contrast with their earlier indifference toward worldly goods. In the family circle, the community and the state they must discard their primitive attitude of aloofness and learn to fellowship their heathen as well as their Christian associates. Since the functions of government were indispensable to society's good order, Christians must lay aside scruples about taking the customary oath of office and indeed seek rather than avoid public responsibilities. Cultural heritages in the form of art, literature, or philosophy were also highly prized by society, and here too Christians had to learn the lesson of accommodation and appreciation. Not until they were prepared to sponsor those interests which gentile society had long regarded as essential to human welfare, and had thought capable of being preserved only by the protection of heaven, could the new religion attain its social triumph. Since human values were under the care of the gods, when Christians became concrete exponents and creators of these values, Gentiles were ready to believe that the God of the Christians was capable of assuming responsibility for the well-being of Roman society.

Thus the day finally arrived when Christianity alone was entrusted with the task that the older religions had failed to accomplish. Religion was still the divine protectress of human values, and, as before, society continued to profit—and to suffer—by adherence to this ancient theory. Charitable activities and humanitarian attitudes were very significantly accelerated under the inspiration of the new faith, but the fundamental structure of society remained essentially unaffected. Christian emperors were no more active than their heathen predecessors had been in promulgating social reforms. Slavery continued to be tolerated and became a recognized Christian institution. Economic inequalities were as much in evidence as ever, and there was no serious effort so to reconstitute society as to remove the underlying causes of trouble. Christian energies were exerted to alleviate distress and prevent flagrant outbreaks of evil, rather than to reform the existing social order. Nor could more have been expected in an age when human values were thoroughly subordinated to divine concerns.

II. *Christianity and Worldly Goods*

II

Christianity and Worldly Goods

THE ATTAINMENT OF FINANCIAL STABILITY IN ROMAN SO-
ciety was a long and arduous task for Christians. The
earliest representatives of the new religion were nota-
bly lacking in worldly possessions. This fact seemed
to cause them no great anxiety, nor did they manifest
any eagerness to improve their economic status. Apparently they neither despised nor coveted the prosperity of their more affluent neighbors. With property as
such they had relatively no concern; their interests
centered in a quite different realm of values.

The first Christian preachers summoned their hearers to prepare for the impending day of Judgment,
when all earthly goods would perish. At present the
business of primary importance was to lay up treasure
in heaven. For the moment one made use of such material things as were available, but attempts systematically to conserve or increase one's personal property
were not thought necessary. The wiser course was to
separate oneself as completely as possible from all en-
tangling alliances with worldly pursuits. Jesus had left
his workshop in Nazareth; Peter and his companions
had given up their business as fishermen; Matthew had
forsaken his post at the customs office; and the early
missionaries had sought no material reward for their
labors. Providence was trusted to furnish such tempo-

41

rary means of subsistence as might be needed until Christ should come to inaugurate his kingdom.

The group of believers that assembled in Jerusalem after the death of Jesus was so indifferent toward the acquisition of material goods that presently its members found themselves sorely pressed to maintain a bare existence. The persons most prominent in the company were peasants and fisherfolk and manual laborers from Galilee who, when their common resources were exhausted, found it difficult to eke out a livelihood in an unaccustomed urban environment. Occasionally a new convert was able to supplement their diminishing funds, and Paul collected a contribution for them from the more prosperous churches established by him on gentile soil. Even thus early the Jerusalem community was known as "the poor" (Gal. 2:10), or "the poor saints" (Rom. 15:26). When finally these Christians were forced to leave Jerusalem on account of the Jewish revolt against Rome in 66-70 A.D., they settled beyond the Jordan and became the ancestors of the sect called the "poor"—the Ebionites.

It was in gentile lands that the economic destiny of Christianity was to be finally determined. Paul never asked new converts to abandon their former means of earning a livelihood or to rid themselves of all material possessions. When sometimes they drew the easy inference that belief in Christ's early advent made it unnecessary for those who possessed a moderate competence to strive for further acquisitions, or when indigent persons were disposed to rely for support upon

42

the generosity of the brotherhood, Paul protested against the procedure. The welfare of the Christian community would be more seriously menaced by the idleness of its members than by their continuance in former callings. Although Paul was confident that the time was short and the Lord was at hand, it was not the task of the Christian preacher to anticipate the divine action by trying to reform the current industrial situation before the Day of Judgment dawned. The converts were to remain in the same occupations in which they had been engaged before joining the church. Christianity for the moment was designed to confer an individual rather than a social good; since God tolerated the present order, Christians would do likewise, whether they were slaves, masters, housewives married to heathen husbands, artisans, traders, or persons engaged in any one of the multiplicity of occupations characteristic of Roman society.

Evidently the Pauline churches had not drawn into their membership any considerable number of the more prosperous people. Yet these gentile Christian communities were financially self-sufficient. They were able also to contribute to the needs of the poor church at Jerusalem, to send Paul funds at critical periods in his life, and to provide for the support of their ministers. Indeed, the Corinthians seem to have felt complimented by the opportunity to have the services of paid preachers, whom they were disposed to rate above Paul because he had labored at secular tasks in order that he might not be a burden to his Corinthian con-

43

verts.[1] His enemies in Corinth had plausibly charged that Paul was not a genuine apostle, else he would have exercised the right to receive financial remuneration for his services to this church. Paul affirmed the right, but explained his divergent practice at Corinth on personal grounds. Thus it is apparent, even in the time of Paul, that among gentile Christians, contrary to Jewish rabbinical custom, labor in the ministry as well as in secular callings was a proper means of earning a livelihood.

I

In the generation after Paul gentile Christendom became more acutely conscious of a concern with worldly goods. When the account of Jesus' teaching and the story of the early church were cast into a form thought suitable for Greek readers having the social standing of a Theophilus, the writer took especial pains to recall incidents and statements that had a definite bearing on economic matters. The new religion now had within the circle of its influence persons representing a comparatively wide range of occupations yielding a regular income. The teaching of John the Baptist was extended to include instruction appropriate to those who had a surplus of clothing and food that might be shared with the needy. Men in the employ of the government, like tax collectors and soldier police, also were recognized as proper seekers for guidance from the new religion

[1] I Cor. 4:12; 9:3-18; II Cor. 11:7-9; I Thess. 2:9; II Thess. 3:8; Acts 18:3.

44

(Luke 3:10-14). Army officers, such as Cornelius of Cæsarea, who could entertain at dinner an impecunious traveling evangelist, were accorded a welcome within the church (Acts, Chap. 10). Incidents of this type were clearly indicative of the fact that during the last quarter of the first century the number of people of moderate means who were inclined to attach themselves to the Christian congregations was gradually on the increase.

Christian leaders, however, had no intention of allowing the church to become a company of the well-to-do. As yet they had not learned to prize the heightened prestige that might thereby accrue to a Christian community in Roman society. Also they viewed with outspoken disapproval the tendency within the Christian groups to yield that deference to men of means which was generally accorded them in the world at large. Christianity was still the rightful possession of the poor; the rich man was something of an interloper. Although converts had been won from among the more prosperous, they were enjoined to dispossess themselves of their worldly goods if they wished to become genuine Christians. They were repeatedly reminded that Jesus had demanded the giving up of all that one possessed as the condition of admission to the Kingdom; they must sell their property and distribute the proceeds among the poor.[2]

[2] This note is especially pronounced in Luke and Acts, as O. Cone, *Rich and Poor in the New Testament* (New York, 1902), pp. 118-158, has clearly shown.

The rich were warned of the snares that wealth set in the pathway to the attainment of worthy moral and spiritual life; they were admonished to keep in mind the approaching Judgment when their worldly possessions would perish; and they were given a glowing picture of the destruction to overtake the industries and luxuries, the trade and the commerce, and all the quests for material goods that so conspicuously marked the life of the Roman world by which they were environed.[3]

By the close of the first century many Christians had become keenly sensitive to economic problems. The older attitude of indifference had given way to two opposite tendencies that now displayed themselves more or less conspicuously in different Christian communities. Some Christian teachers still idealized the impecunious status of the early Christian groups and exalted this condition to the authority of a standard valid for all time; poverty was necessary to righteousness. But the very vehemence displayed in advocating this ideal is unmistakable testimony to the presence of a strong counter tendency within the Christian communities looking toward a more stable economic position. At first this more worldly disposition did not parade itself as an ideal, and elicited no oratory on its behalf; but it was irresistibly motivated by the actual conditions under which men found themselves living. Christianity had now reached a stage where, if it were to endure, it must strike its roots more deeply into the

[3] For example, I Tim. 6:7-19; James 5:1-8; Rev., Chap. 18.

soil of contemporary economic life. Its members must give themselves more diligently to worldly business, even when this was done under the protest of leaders and perhaps also with a feeling of self-disapproval on the part of the individual. But with changing circumstances idealistic thinking gradually found new modes of expression better suited to the actualities of the new situation.

Henceforth the gap between the teaching of Christian idealists with respect to the accumulation and use of material goods, and the practice of individual members in the church, was sometimes a wide one.[4] Frequently the teaching was far in advance of, or lagged far behind, the actual practice, according to one's point

[4] The teachings of the early church on labor, occupations, and property have been assembled in detail by C. J. Cadoux, *The Early Church and the World* (Edinburgh, 1925) in the various sections on "Property" scattered through the volume; I. Seipel, *Die wirtschaftsethischen Lehren der Kirchenväter* (Theologische Studien der Leo-Gesellschaft, No. 18, Wien, 1907); O. Schilling, *Reichtum und Eigentum in der altchristlichen Literatur* (Freiburg i. Br., 1908); F. Hauck, *Die Stellung des Urchristentums zu Arbeit und Geld* (Gütersloh, 1921); U. Benigni, *Storia sociale della chiesa,* Vol. I (Milano, 1906), pp. 319-424. Briefer treatments are given by V. Bartlet, "The Biblical and Early Christian Idea of Property," in the composite volume *Property, Its Rights and Duties* (Second edition, New York, 1922); O. Cone, *Rich and Poor in the New Testament* (New York, 1902); A. Bigelmair, *Die Beteiligung der Christen am öffentlichen Leben in vorconstantinischer Zeit* (München, 1902), pp. 293-321; E. Troeltsch, *Die sociallehren der christlichen Kirchen und Gruppen* (Tübingen, 1912), pp. 113-134, now available in an English rendering, *The Social Teaching of the Christian Churches* (New York, 1931). Further data about occupations, not extensively used by the previously mentioned writers, may be obtained from archeological remains, for which see C. M. Kaufmann, *Handbuch der altchristliche Epigraphik* (Freiburg i. Br., 1917), pp. 106-117; E. Diehl, *Inscriptiones latinae christianae veteres,* Vol. I (Berlin, 1925), Nos. 347-807.

47

of view. The preacher might warn or threaten or plead with his hearers to renounce all worldly concerns and if need be to starve to death rather than come to terms with the alleged demonic order by which he found himself surrounded in his ordinary daily living. But the average Christian could not shake off the power of his will to live materially as well as spiritually; and when compromise with ideals became necessary to keep soul and body together, he found it possible to make the necessary adjustments. Often the idealists' condemnation of one or another occupation or profession is a clear indication of the fact that members of the church were already to be found in these callings and believed it proper to remain therein in order to perpetuate their existence and attain to the recognition and respect which they felt was their due in the society of the time.

It was inevitable, however, that Christians should view with horror and disgust the luxury and attendant immorality of the rich in their heathen environment. So long as affluence and profligacy seemed inseparable, Christians spurned wealth as the inevitable concomitant of wickedness. In the sight of God, the goods of the material world, along with the characteristic uses to which riches ministered, were thought to merit utter condemnation. Christian teachers, who at the larger centers of population saw all about them the extravagances and evil practices to which heathen prosperity lent itself, were vehement in their condemnation of luxurious living. At Rome, Carthage, Alexandria, An-

48

tioch, and other cities, the society of the wealthy presented to the moral sensitivities of Christians a hideous exhibition of intolerable evils.[5]

Wanton displays of wealth met one on every hand. Upon the streets men and women appeared robed in fine raiment and bedecked with gold ornaments and precious gems. At the public festivities one witnessed lavish expenditures to gratify a momentary lust for pleasure. Enormous sums were spent on feasts where rare foods and costly wines were consumed from jewel-embossed dishes, and revelry knew no bounds. Homes were adorned with luxurious furnishings to satisfy the mere vanity of the owner. Hordes of slaves were kept for the purpose of flagrantly displaying the master's wealth. Idle ladies, borne about in litters on the shoulders of their menials, had no aims in life but to visit and gossip with their equally indolent neighbors. No one turned his hand to the smallest kind of useful labor; a slave was always at one's elbow to render every motion of the master or mistress unnecessary. The Christian observer could see nothing to praise, but everything to condemn, in this sordid display of selfishness and ostentation. Even though he were himself a person of cultivated tastes, he could more readily admire the barbarian simplicity of life exemplified by the Celts and Scythians. Clement intimated that it

[5] The vanities of wealth in Rome are reflected in various places in the *Shepherd of Hermas*; Clement of Alexandria in his *Exhortation* and in his *Instructor* criticizes the display of luxury in that city; and similar phenomena in Carthage call forth sharp protests from Tertullian and Cyprian.

might be said of some of the rich men in Alexandria that "his horse is worth fifteen talents, or his field, or his domestic, or his gold, but the man himself is dear at three coppers."[6]

Little wonder that Christians, themselves often on the verge of starvation amid the luxurious extravagance seen on every hand about them, should often have thought worldly goods to be in and of themselves an unmitigated evil. Only slowly did a more discriminating estimate of values emerge. Luxury and worldliness still met with vigorous disapproval, but in time it dawned upon Christians that the possession of property did not necessarily compel one to live an evil life. Prosperity could be made to serve worthy religious ends. Gradually during the second century this conviction increased, as converts were secured in larger numbers from among the well-to-do members of society who rendered valuable service to the Christian cause.

The church at Rome even before the year 100 had gratefully counted in its membership some rich men who helped the poor, and for whose existence the needy man blessed God.[7] In those Christian circles where the Pastoral Epistles were composed for the instruction and guidance of church leaders, young bishops were advised to encourage the rich to be high-minded in good works by ministering to the needs of the poor.[8] Even among those Christians at Rome who culti-

[6] *Instructor,* III. 6.   [7] I Clement, xxxviii.   [8] I Tim. 6:17-19.

vated ascetic ideals and urged the faithful to rid themselves of their worldly possessions, the desirability of acquiring and retaining a moderate competence as a basis for continued and regular almsgiving received encouragement. These were good, although not the best, Christians, whose property God had not taken away completely, in order that they might be able to serve his cause by means of the possessions which they had been allowed to retain.[9] Contribution to the common fund used by the church in relieving the needs of the poor was a fundamental Christian duty, but it was maintained on a purely voluntary basis and was not so extremely pressed as to kill the goose that laid the golden egg.[10] The love of money, not its mere possession, was the root of evil. In the case of the rich who hoarded their wealth and refused to help the needy, prophecy would be fulfilled: "that which the saints have not eaten the Assyrians shall eat, and strangers shall devour their land before their eyes."[11]

Christians of a more philosophic turn of mind justified prosperity not only on grounds of utility, but as a divine right. After all, had not their God created the material world and pronounced good the work of his hands? It was he who had made the winds for man's service, rendering possible traffic upon the sea and the transport of foodstuffs and other commodities needful

---

[9] Shepherd of Hermas, *Similitudes,* II. 5-10; IX. 30. 5.
[10] Note Justin, *Apology,* i. 14 f.; Tertullian, *Apology,* xxxix, 4 f.
[11] *Didascalia,* xvii; cf. Isa. 1:7.

for mankind.[12] Plato had said that the goods of friends are shared in common, and since God and Christians are the closest of friends, all the beneficent works of his creation might rightfully be claimed as a proper Christian possession. It was God who had provided a fertile soil for men to cultivate, water for them to drink and to navigate, air for them to breathe, fire to serve their needs, and a world in which their lives could be sustained. The Christian would till his fields, keeping God always in mind. He would avail himself of the privileges offered by the means of navigation, giving heed always to the will of the Heavenly Pilot. If converted while engaged in military service, he would remain at his post but yield his mind to the orders of the Divine Commander. "The entire life of men who have come to know Christ is good."[13]

This was the type of teaching advocated by the Christian scholars of Alexandria at the end of the second century. The ascetic note was somewhat more prominent in the West, yet the same disposition to regard property as a rightful Christian possession in accordance with God's creative goodness was not lacking at Rome and Carthage. Christians in Asia also had become like-minded. Origen at Cæsarea per-

[12] Aristides, *Apology*, v.

[13] Clement of Alexandria, *Exhortation*, X. 100. 4; XI. 115. 1; XII. 122. 3; 123. 1. See also the fragment of the so-called *Preaching of Peter*, which affirms that God by the act of creation had given all things to mankind, and therefore the rich ought to imitate the divine generosity and share their abundance with the poor; cited by M. R. James, *The Apocryphal New Testament* (Oxford, 1924), p. 19.

52

petuated the teaching he had learned at Alexandria. People generally at this time were crediting prosperity to the divine favor for the imperial regime and acknowledging their gratitude by rendering worship to the ruler and the old deities who were assumed to sponsor his administration. The Christian offered a different interpretation. He affirmed that it was his God, and not the earthly king, who guaranteed prosperity. All possessions acquired properly and honorably came from the true God through the generosity of his providence. He had created fruits and grain for man's sustenance, as well as the pleasant vine and wine which, in the words of the Psalmist, rejoiced the heart of man. Even olive oil, one of the chief commodities of profitable trade in the Roman world, and indispensable to the toilet of the well-groomed person, was derived from the providence of God.[14]

Two important influences affecting the growth of Christianity in the second century had contributed significantly to the new Christian way of evaluating worldly goods. One incentive came from the heathen world itself, while the other was inspired by Christianity's heritage from Judaism. Leaders like Tertullian of Carthage and Clement of Alexandria brought into the service of the church ways of thinking that had been shaped under the tutelage of Stoicism, which held that the material world was by nature good. Evil

[14] Origen, *Celsus*, VIII. 67. Similarly, Lactantius declares the Stoics to be correct in teaching that the world had been made for man's use (*Anger of God*, xiii. 1).

53

was due to man's perversion of an order of existence originally generated in conformity with the divine reason. By nature the universe was good; evil was an intruder. In the second place, the Gnostics, who caused the church much trouble during the second century, had pushed their doctrine of the inherently evil character of matter to so extreme a limit that the fundamental importance of the Old Testament Scriptures in the life of the Christian communities was seriously menaced. When followed to its logical conclusion, Gnostic teaching made the God of the Hebrew revelation an inferior Deity, if not indeed an evil demon. But the Scriptures were too thoroughly intrenched in the life of the Christian assemblies, and too valuable as an ancient source of authority for the Christian apologist, to be sacrificed to Gnostic doubts. Hence it became incumbent upon Christian leaders to think more highly than had formerly been their custom of the material world that God himself had created.

The new mode of thinking became increasingly valuable to the Christian cause as the number of its well-to-do members multiplied. Spiritual values remained supreme, and the quest for worldly goods was always to be made subservient to moral and religious ideals, but a moderate prosperity was no longer inconsistent with the aims of the church. The manner by which material possessions were acquired and the ways in which they were to be used now became the focal points of chief concern to the Christian moralists. One who cherished his possessions, whether of gold or sil-

54

ver or houses, as gifts from God, and used his substance to help the needy friends of God, rather than for his own selfishness and pleasure, enjoyed full divine approval. He was the man whom the Lord had called "poor in spirit."[15]

By the close of the second century the church had learned for all time to come the desirability of having at its command a substantial body of this world's goods. Such could be made available only as Christians enjoyed a larger measure of prosperity. The older attitude of indifference or hostility to material possessions now gave way to a new form of idealism which inculcated industry and frugality among Christians, who were to cherish their possessions in order that they might make substantial and regular contributions toward the needs of the church. Preachers no longer railed against the rich, declaring it impossible for them to be saved, but welcomed them into the church on condition that they consecrate both themselves and their financial resources to the service of Christ. The famous discourse on this theme by Clement of Alexandria, although composed over seventeen centuries ago, might be repeated today from the pulpit of the most wealthy church without fear of giving offense to the richest member of the congregation.[16] Speaking in the temper of Seneca rather than of Jesus, Clement

[15] Clement of Alexandria, *Rich Man's Salvation,* 16.

[16] This sermon is available in convenient form in G. W. Butterworth, *Clement of Alexandria* (New York, 1929), a volume in the Loeb Classical Library. There is an older translation in the Ante-Nicene Fathers, Vol. II (New York, 1885), pp. 589-604.

55

declared that "wealth rightly used renders service to righteousness, while wrongly used it is a servant of unrighteousness; for by nature its function is to serve, not to rule. . . . So let no one do away with his property, but rather with the passions of his soul, which do not assent to the better use of his possessions, in order that on becoming noble and good (*i.e.,* on becoming a Christian) he may be able to use nobly this property. Accordingly, the command 'to renounce all they possess' (Luke 14:33) and 'to sell all they possess' (Matt. 19:21) is to be understood as having been spoken with reference to the passions of the soul" (Chap. 14).

II

By their insistence upon the dignity and necessity of work, Christian idealists contributed in no slight degree to undermine prejudice against the possession of property. The industrious life was encouraged within gentile Christianity from the start. Paul's warning to the Thessalonians against giving free food to any man who refused to work[17] was often repeated in later times. This did not mean that work was enjoined as a Christian virtue, but rather that it was a practical necessity for the maintenance of the community's life. In a society originally composed of people of very moderate means, who were at the same time devoted to the ideals of brotherhood and charity, it was quite impracticable to cherish in its midst idlers who were capable

[17] II Thess. 3:10.

56

of engaging in profitable employment. Everyone must toil with his hands according to his ability in order to make himself a useful member of the community.

By their attitude toward work Christians did much to dignify a form of activity that was generally looked upon with disdain by cultured people in the Roman world. In a society where manual labor was performed mainly by slaves, and where the modern machine in industry was unknown, the man who was compelled to toil with his hands merited but slight respect. The situation of even the free laborer might be less fortunate and dignified than that of a slave in the employ of a capable master. But in the Christian group these outward social relationships were a secondary consideration. Slaves, free laborers, and masters became members of a new brotherhood where all were said to be equal in the sight of God. The laborer was not thereby relieved of the necessity of work. In fact, Christianity taught the slave that he ought to be more faithful and conscientious in the discharge of his duties just because he had become a Christian. If he were an official in the church, where his master might be only an ordinary member of the congregation, the slave was not to forget that outside of the Christian community his obligation to his master remained unaltered.[18]

[18] Clement of Alexandria remarked that Christians, having been redeemed from the worst bondage, were good to their domestics (*Exhortation*, X. 107. 3). Further, "domestics ought to be treated like ourselves, for they are human beings as we are; 'for, if you stop to think, all men—those who are free and those who are slaves—have the same God' "

57

Laborers who did not belong to the slave class must often have been at a great disadvantage in seeking opportunities to earn a livelihood in Roman society. Many of them early became members of the church. It would have been quite contrary to the dictates of human nature if some of these new converts had not been tempted to take an unfair advantage of the privileges of brotherhood and charity made available for them in their new association. In order to protect itself the church had to become virtually an employment bureau engaged in the task of finding work for its idle members. If a man had a trade an effort was made to place him in an occupation where he could use his accumulated knowledge and skill. But even if this position could not be found he was in duty bound to take such other employment as might be secured for him by the church. Only for those indigent members of the brotherhood who were physically incapable of toil, or were temporarily unable to find any employment, did the church undertake to provide food and shelter.[19]

The practical necessity, which made it desirable for

(*Instructor*, III. 12. 92). Possibly the last sentence is a quotation from the Stoic poet Menander. In this connection Clement also repeated typical New Testament passages demanding kindness from masters and respectful obedience from slaves. These sentiments had been frequently expressed in earlier times—*e.g.* Gal. 3:28; 4:1, 7; I Cor. 7:21; 12:13; Philemon 10-20; Col. 3:11; 3:22-4:1; Eph. 6:5-9; I Tim. 6:1 f.; Tit. 2:9; *Didache*, IV. 10-12; Ignatius, *To Polycarp*, 4. For Roman slavery in general, see R. M. Barrow, *Slavery in the Roman Empire* (London, 1928); and for the position of slaves in Christianity, P. Allard, *Les esclaves chrétiens* (6th edition, Paris, 1914).

[19] *Didache*, XII. 3.

all church members to be earners, had very significant consequences for the social integration of Christianity. On the one hand, it dignified the lot of the laboring-man. He now felt himself in fellowship with Jesus, who had been a carpenter, with Peter who had been a fisherman, with Paul who had been a tent-maker, and even with God himself who had labored six days in the creation of the world. Also this new status of the toiler made possible a greater sense of security and freedom from misfortune amid the uncertainties of daily ex-perience. If suddenly thrown out of employment, or incapacitated by sickness, one did not immediately be-come a social derelict, but found in the Christian brotherhood those who were ready to help in the hour of need. The poor Christian was given a respectable burial if he died, or if his sickness were not unto death he could be sure of assistance during his period of ill-ness, and on recovering his health he could confidently expect to be furnished with future employment through the kind offices of his fellow Christians. This activity of the Christian church must have exerted a strong influence upon the social solidification of its own membership.

Another result, quite as important for the growth of Christianity's influence, was the gradual permeation of society by Christian laborers. As the membership of the groups multiplied Christians were to be found in a great variety of occupations and professions. For many years the chief acquisitions to the new religion were adult converts, who were accustomed to earn a

59

livelihood in standard ways and who continued in their former positions. Other converts who had no employment were compelled to accept such as could be found. Practical necessity extended the range of these operations far beyond any schedule of legitimate callings that even the most liberally minded idealist might at any given time have formulated as proper for Christians. Economic maintenance was the primary consideration, and in a society where employment was mainly at the disposal of the heathen, it would have been futile for Christians to have attempted any extensive limitation in the range of work suitable for a recent convert. One could not avoid idolatrous associations even when engaged in the least objectionable kinds of labor. The wide range of activities in which Christians were ultimately to be found earning their livelihood caused some Christian teachers, like the rigorous Tertullian, much anxiety. They tried to set up rules with reference to the kinds of work in which one might continue and yet be admitted to the church, and to prescribe the occupations and professions legitimate for members who wished to remain in good standing. This effort to remedy a situation that had grown up quite spontaneously was by no means always successful, as the Christian teachers themselves recognized.

At the outset the moral ideals of Christianity affected the laborer more in respect to the character of the service which he sought to render than in the choice which he made of an occupation. Unalterable circumstances must often have determined his calling quite apart from any personal tastes. On the other hand, the ideals of fidelity and honesty which he exemplified in the discharge of his duties were subject to his own will and provided an area in which he could demonstrate his Christian character. For example, in the case of slaves a choice of work was out of the question. From the Christian point of view, to run away from the master would be a kind of thievery by which an owner would be deprived of his rightful property. So to act would have been a violation of Christian ethical standards. What the master required of the slave had to be done. But the Christian slave could perform his duties by a higher standard still; he worked not only for his earthly master, but for the glory and approval of God. Even when forced to perform acts intimately associated with heathenism, the slave still cherished Christ in his heart and sought to exhibit in his conduct the worthiest type of honesty and fidelity. Owners of slaves and employers of free labor in the Roman world would have been dull indeed had they not soon discovered that it was distinctly to their advantage to have in their service workers who were members of the Christian churches.

In both the East and the West, before the close of the second century, Christianity had spread widely among the working-classes and small tradespeople of the Empire, where Christians constituted one of the most industrious and dependable elements in the population. Without fear of effective refutation they declared their own essential worth to the existing social order. Shortly after the middle of the second century a Christian apologist in Rome could boast that the new religion included among its converts representatives of a wide range of activities. One found in the church not only philosophers and rhetoricians, but also skilled workmen, as well as persons of no education whatsoever.[20] In this statement the Christian philosopher was perhaps unduly complimentary to his own sect. A generation later Clement of Alexandria somewhat more modestly remarked that Christian teaching had spread world-wide, winning converts "from every nation and village and city, already bringing over to the truth whole households as well as private individuals, and indeed not a few of the philosophers themselves."[21] Undoubtedly the more common opinion was expressed by the Roman critic who resented the claim of Christians to be teachers of true religion when they were people "devoid of learning, strangers to education, and unskilled in even the most humble forms of artisanship."[22] While this deprecatory pronouncement hardly did full justice to the personnel of the Christian communities in the closing decades of the second century, doubtless it was relatively correct. A few persons of education and dignity were now to be found in the churches, but certainly the majority were slaves, com-

[20] Justin, *Apology*, II. 10. 8.
[21] *Stromateis*, VI. 18. 167.
[22] Minucius Felix, *Octavius*, V. 4.

62

mon laborers, and people without recognized social standing according to the ideas of that age.

The situation was, however, exceedingly significant for Christianity's success. It meant that the new religion was striking at the very roots of the social structure by penetrating widely into the life of the workaday world. Opponents recognized this fact and condemned Christianity all the more vigorously on this account. It seemed to them like a dangerous malady that was stealthily undermining the social health. One scathing critic in the East thus described the menace: "We see in private houses workers in wool and cobblers and fullers and the most uneducated and rustic people who do not dare to open their mouths in the presence of their more worthy and intelligent masters; but when they find the children alone, and certain ignorant women with them, they deliver themselves of some wonderful utterances declaring that it is not necessary to heed the father and the teachers, but to obey them (the Christians). Indeed, they say that the father and the teachers, who indulge in silly talk and are weak-minded, are able neither to possess nor to know nor to do that which is worthy, since they have been ensnared by empty nonsense. The Christians alone know how one ought to live, and if the children will obey them they will be happy themselves and will render the home happy."[23] The same critic, speaking of the class of people to whom Christianity appealed, added: "Whoever is a sinner, they say, whoever

[23] Origen, *Celsus,* III. 55.

63

is unwise, whoever is untaught, in brief, whoever is wretched, him will the kingdom of heaven receive."[24]

At this stage in its growth the defenders of Christianity conceded that its membership had been drawn largely from among the uncultured classes. While its teaching was in reality a divine philosophy, in its earthly manifestation it was essentially a way of living to be pursued by persons engaged in many humble callings within Roman society. But the popular charge that their presence was detrimental to the common good was vigorously refuted. Instead of admitting that they were useless or harmful to the world, Christians declared themselves to be the new saving leaven dispersed throughout society for its salvation.

As one apologist, whose name is no longer known, expressed it, "Christians are not differentiated from the rest of mankind either by country, language, or customs. For they neither dwell in any cities of their own, nor employ any unusual dialect, nor practice any strange mode of life. Nor do they possess the kind of knowledge that is discovered by any device and ingenuity of inquisitive men; nor are they, like some, advocates of human philosophic dogma. While they dwell in both Greek and non-Greek cities, according to individual circumstances, and follow native customs in clothing and food and other phases of life, yet they set forth a marvelous and confessedly incredible type of citizenship for themselves. They live in their native

[24] *Ibid.*, III. 59.

64

countries, but as sojourners; they participate in all activities as citizens, and endure all things as strangers. Every foreign land is their fatherland, and every fatherland is foreign. They marry like all other men and beget children, but they do not expose their offspring. They share a common table, but not a common bed.[25] They are in the flesh, but do not live according to the flesh. They abide on earth, but live as citizens of heaven. They obey the established laws, and in their own lives they surpass the laws. They love all men and are persecuted by all. They are unrecognized, and yet they are condemned. They are put to death, and they have an increase of life. They are poor, yet they bestow riches on many. They suffer the want of all things, and they superabound in all things. They endure indignities, and they are glorified in their indignities. They are slandered, and they are justified. They are abused, and they bless. They are scoffed at and they show reverence. While they perform good deeds they are punished as evildoers. When punished they rejoice as attaining unto life. They are warred against as aliens by the Jews and are persecuted by the Greeks, yet those who hate them are unable to state the cause of their hatred. In brief, what the soul is to the body Christians are to the world. As the soul is dispersed throughout all the members of the body, so Christians are scattered among all the cities of the

---

[25] Similarly Tertullian, *Apology,* xxxix. 11: "All things are without distinction among us, except wives."

65

world. The soul resides in the body but is not of the body, and Christians reside in the world but are not of the world."[26]

In their struggle for a livelihood converts to Christianity had as yet been unable to separate themselves from customary industrial activities, even had they been disposed so to do. The rites of heathen worship and participation in gross immoralities were no longer permitted to them, but in all other affairs they mingled freely in the society of the day. That this was the situation in North Africa shortly before the year 200 is clearly revealed in Tertullian's *Apology*, even though personally he would have advised Christians to exercise a much greater reserve in respect to their daily contacts. He contended that in only one particular was there any truth in the popular accusation that Christians were a menace to the economic interests of society. It was an admitted fact that they made no contribution to the revenues of the temples, yet they helped the needy by means of their generous almsgiving. It was also true that they bought no incense to burn before the images of the gods, yet they purchased large quantities of this commodity for use in the burial of the Christian dead. But apart from their religious exclusiveness, it was absurd to allege that Christians were an economic detriment to society because useless in the work and business of the Roman world. "How can

---

[26] *Epistle to Diognetus,* V f. The treatise is written in Greek, probably toward the close of the second century, and seems to have more particularly in view the situation in the East.

this be true," exclaims Tertullian, "of persons who are living in your very midst, subsisting on the same food, using the same clothing, following the same customs, and busied with the same things necessary for the maintenance of life?" Christians live in a world which their God has created and they feel entitled to the full use of all its material blessings, if at the same time they are careful to practice moderation and honesty. Hence, continues Tertullian, "we dwell with you in this world, renouncing neither forum, nor meat-market, nor baths, stores, workshops, taverns, fairs and other places of commerce. We sail with you upon the sea and with you we serve in the army, work on the land, and carry on trade. Indeed, we practice handicrafts, furnishing the public with our products for your use. I do not understand how we seem useless in your business affairs with which and from which we live."[27]

Writing in Gaul, where Christianity had won many converts before the close of the second century, Irenæus implied that numerous employments were legitimate for Christians, if not indeed already engaged in by members of the church. Although he was speaking

[27] Tertullian, *Apology,* xlii. 1-3. It is a popular outcry in Tertullian's day that the state is being overrun by Christians. They are "in the fields, in the fortresses, in the islands; and it is lamented as a calamity that persons of both sexes, of all ages, of every condition, and even of every class, join this movement." *Apology,* i. 7. Again in xxxvii. 4: "We are of yesterday and already we have filled the world and all your places—cities, islands, fortresses, municipalities, market-places, the camp itself, the tribes, the decuries, the palace, the senate, the forum. We have left you only your temples."

ideally, it seems improbable that he would have taken pains to list so many types of worldly activity as worthy had not orthodox Christians been pursuing some of these callings. Refuting those sectaries who justified worldliness on the ground that the soul should seek every type of experience in order to secure freedom from the necessity of further incarnations, Irenæus alleged that the Gnostics did not really engage in those pursuits which "pertain to virtue, and are laborious and glorious and demand skill, and which are also universally approved as good." Irenæus' catalog of worthy activities includes music, arithmetic, geometry, astronomy, and intellectual disciplines in general. Medicine and study of plants used in treating human ills are also commended;[28] likewise, painting and sculpture and skilled workmanship in brass, marble, and kindred materials. Farming, treatment of animal ailments, tending flocks, and skilled labor required generally for the maintenance of life, are good as are the arts of maritime life, gymnastics, hunting, and service in the army and under rulers. The heretics, says Irenæus, will not be found thus profitably occupied. It is vain for them to boast that in their discipleship to Jesus they are engaged in activities contributing to "the benefit and stability of mankind." One readily infers that orthodox Christians, if not already extensively engaged in these "good" works, certainly re-

---

[28] Among the Christians put to death in Gaul during the persecution of 177 A.D. there was a Phrygian physician, Alexander, who had been a resident of Gaul for many years. Eusebius, *History,* V. 1. 49.

68

garded such forms of employment as entirely proper and desirable.[29]

An exhaustive list of the various occupations and professions in which Christians were to be found at any specific moment in the history of ancient Christianity is not at present available. Were complete statistics accessible, doubtless one would find members of the church engaged at one time or another in all the various activities by which people in the Roman world were accustomed to earn an honorable livelihood. Gentile Christianity gained its foothold first in the cities and among the lower strata of society. Slaves were conspicuous among its early adherents, yet their contribution to its economic success was in the nature of the case rather limited. But converts from among manual laborers, skilled artisans, and small traders, of the freedman and freeman class, were also numerous at an early date; and their earning ability was measurably increased and stabilized as a result of membership in the new association. Their numbers multiplied rapidly with the spread of the Christian movement throughout the Roman Empire.

A survey of the Christian inscriptions reveals, sometimes by the pictures of the instruments sketched on the tombstones and often by specific designations, the kind of occupation in which the deceased had been engaged. Here we meet, for example, barbers, hog-killers, bakers, corn-grinders, confectioners, cooks,

---

[29] Irenæus, *Heresies,* II. 49. 1 f. in the edition of Harvey; II. 32. 2 f. in Stieren.

69

waiters, chambermen and chambermaids, hostlers, chariot-drivers, gardeners, vine-dressers, shepherds, storehouse-keepers, clothes-checkers, rag-dealers, builders of couches and cabinets and chariots, physicians, veterinaries, mule doctors, midwives, nurses, grave-diggers; dealers in clothing, fruit, incense, charcoal, meat, fish, olive oil, stationery, ivory; cobblers, linen and wool workers, clothes-repairers, mirror-makers, workers in ivory, gold and silver smiths, braziers, potters, locksmiths, blacksmiths; miners, stone-cutters, marble-workers, bas-relief-makers, architects, masons, carpenters, painters, artists; bank clerks, money-changers, tax-collectors, bill-collectors, cashiers, coin-makers, treasurers, secretaries, stenographers, copyists, keepers of records, patrons, tutors, defensors, advocates; schoolmasters, grammarians, rhetoricians, teachers of Greek, teachers of Latin; trainers of performers at the spectacles, rope-makers, chorus-masters, chariot-repairers, keepers of the horses, gymnasts, dancers, trumpeters, entertainers; sailors, soldiers, military officers of various ranks, bodyguards, stewards, superintendents; makers of armor, swords, spears, arrows; magistrates and other civic officials.

III

The total result of continued years of Christian industry and frugality was the emergence of a religious community in which many of the members became well-to-do, while the church itself grew to be an important financial institution. As early as the second

70

decade of the second century Christianity had penetrated so deeply into the social life of the imperial province of Bithynia-Pontus that the economic resources of the country had been extensively deflected from customary channels. At least, so it seemed to the new governor, Pliny the Younger, whom the Emperor Trajan had recently appointed. Not only slaves and ordinary day laborers had gone over to the Christian religion; also people of means, who had formerly financed the religious and civic enterprises characteristic of a prosperous heathen community, had become adherents of the new religion. It is far from probable that the resources of the province had actually been impaired by the growth of Christianity, which had, as the governor affirms, captured many people of every rank not only in the cities, but also in the villages and country districts. But funds under Christian control were no longer available for the usual purposes. The consequences seemed to Pliny very serious, and he could imagine no way by which the economic resources of the province could be recaptured for the public good except through forcing Christians to return to the heathen mode of life. This, as he was careful to explain to the emperor, was his primary motive in persecuting Christians. Had their economic significance been less important, doubtless they would have remained unmolested.[30]

Another illustration of Christian prosperity in Pontus is furnished in the person of Marcion, a wealthy

[30] Pliny, *Epistles*, X. 96.

71

shipowner from Sinope, who came to Rome about the year 140 and intimately allied himself with the work of the church. He contributed to its budget, if Tertullian's figures are correct, the sum of 200,000 sesterces —over eight thousand dollars.[31] And if a few years later the Roman church was able to return this amount to Marcion, as it is said to have done when he was expelled for doctrinal aberrations, that act was a testimony to its own financial self-sufficiency. Before the close of the second century Christians in Asia were prosperous enough to incite the cupidity of informers who instigated outbreaks against them with the hope of plundering their possessions.[32]

During the third century Christianity made comparatively rapid and extensive gains in the economic sphere. Larger numbers of prosperous people attached themselves to the church and, with the growth in membership, Christians extended their operations more widely in industry and business. All sorts of trade and commerce, which did not involve outright worship of heathen deities or participation in grave immoralities, were now fully accepted as suitable for members of the church, both laity and clergy. At Alexandria, the ethical standards of Clement freely admitted the propriety of Christians' engaging in business affairs, if only they were careful to maintain their moral integrity. The merchant was warned against having two prices

[31] Tertullian, *Against Heretics*, xxx.
[32] This is the statement of Melito, bishop of Sardis, according to Eusebius, *History*, IV. 26. 5.

72

and making false statements about his wares. It was necessary to maintain truthfulness, even though to state the just price at the start and refuse to be beaten down might lose one a customer.[33] Evidently this procedure was quite contrary to the usual methods of trade in that day, as it still is in that part of the world. But Christian tradespeople managed to succeed, while not deviating, at least conspicuously, from Clement's moral principle that there was no place in Christianity for the greedy, the falsifiers, the hypocrites, and those who make merchandise of the truth.

Perhaps it was just this moral ideal, even when followed at a distance, that won the Christian shopkeeper ultimate success. At least he had dependability to his credit so long as he followed the teaching of the church. In the course of time Christians were to be found side by side with the heathen engaging successfully in the big business of the empire. By the close of the third century it was possible for a Christian apologist, when refuting the charge that Christian neglect of the ancient gods had brought distress upon society, to call to the emperor's attention the fact that some Christian merchants had recently grown not only richer, but indeed very wealthy, by trading in foodstuffs during a period of high prices.[34]

By the middle of the third century well-to-do Christians had become so numerous that the confiscation of

[33] Clement of Alexandria, *Instructor*, III. xi. 78. 4.

[34] Arnobius, I. 16: cur ibidem annonaria caritate non tantum corporis non nostri verum etiam christianos ditiores et locupletissimos rediderunt?

73

their goods in the time of persecution made a welcome addition to the government's dwindling income. As the bishop of Carthage looked back upon the Decian persecution of the year 250, which had subsided with the death of the emperor in the summer of the following year, the temporary distress suffered by the church seemed to convey one outstanding lesson. God had let it loose as a warning to Christians that they had been concerned too much with material prosperity, so extensively acquired during the previous decades of comparative freedom from interference by the authorities. Even after due allowance has been made for Cyprian's rhetorical art, one cannot read his treatise, *On the Lapsed,* without becoming acutely aware of the remarkable progress that had been made by Christians in possessing themselves of worldly goods—but at what a tremendous cost to the older Christian ideals of simplicity and otherworldliness!

Cyprian's condemnations were severe and, from his point of view, amply justified. Yet a different evaluation was possible. The Christian man who, setting aside the Levitical injunction,[35] trimmed his beard according to the custom current among his business associates, or the Christian lady who plucked her eyebrows, charcoaled her eyelashes, rouged her cheeks and dyed her hair, in order to be in style in polite society, was prompted by motives that the bishop could hardly be expected to appreciate. The Christian man of means and the members of his family doubtless felt it would

[35] Levit. 19:27.

74

do their religion no credit for them to appear in public dowdy and unkempt, according to the standards of the society within which their economic position now entitled them to move. They need not have felt any less true to the church than do modern Christians when the men don evening dress and the ladies wear their most expensive jewelry to attend a formal social function.

Members of the church who had lapsed in the Decian persecution caused much grief to their more rigorous brethren. But it is not surprising that the glory of martyrdom had lost much of its old appeal for Christians who had become extensively involved in economic activities. Outward conformity to the government's demands would save one's home, family, property, and business, while Christianity still remained the religion of the inner life. To deceive the persecutor was but to fight Satan with his own weapons. One might sacrifice with the tongue in the cheek, so to speak; or might purchase a certificate from a venal magistrate, thus cheating the devil of his prey; or might partake of the required sacrificial meal at the temple, at the same time nullifying its effect by quietly saying the name of Christ; and thereafter pursue unmolested one's usual business in society. When the persecution had passed these persons returned to the church, probably with no serious compunctions of conscience. They still possessed their property and had no wish to forsake Christianity.

It was the prosperity of Christians that made the

75

problem of the lapsed so acute. This fact was clearly perceived by Cyprian, who specifically charged that these persons had "chosen their patrimony in preference to God." They had been deceived and conquered by their wealth. The only effective remedy that Cyprian could propose was complete renunciation: "Property is to be avoided as an enemy, to be fled from as a robber, to be feared by its possessors as a sword and poison."[36] But this admonition was not to prevail. All through the third and fourth centuries many Christians in North Africa continued to be engrossed in worldly business and held substantial material possessions. When Augustine composed his *City of God*, the right of Christians to own property and engage successfully in business was taken for granted by the church. Heathen opposition to Christianity, says Augustine, had broken down in the face of God's manifest favor in allowing Christians to increase and prosper. Hence the church voluntarily approved a quest for the things necessary to humanity's natural existence, in so far as this end could be attained without detriment to piety and godliness.[37]

In Italy a similar course of development had been in progress. Rigor and moderation had come into sharp conflict at Rome during the early decades of the third century, with Hippolytus and Callistus leading, respectively, the two tendencies. Tradition says that as a slave Callistus had once conducted a banking business for a

[36] Cyprian, *On the Lapsed*, 35.
[37] Augustine, *City of God*, XIX. 17.

rich Christian master and had induced his fellow Christians to deposit their money in the institution. Then the bank failed and he became a fugitive, ultimately landing as a convict in the mines of Sardinia. Such is the story told by his bitter enemy, Hippolytus. Whatever the element of truth in this tradition may be, at any rate the church of Rome elevated Callistus rather than Hippolytus to the episcopacy in 217 A.D. Callistus' idea of the church as a community of believers who were on the way to sainthood, in contrast with the view of Hippolytus that this attainment should become a reality before admission to the church was allowed, was certainly the more popular in Rome, where adherents of Christianity were now much involved in affairs of the world.

At Rome, as at Carthage, the more liberal attitude toward secular activities henceforth prevailed. It must have required a prosperous body of members to finance the budget of so large and active an institution as the Roman church was by the middle of the third century, when it had in its service forty-six presbyters, seven deacons, seven sub-deacons, forty-two acolytes, fifty-two exorcists, as well as readers and doorkeepers whose numbers are not specified. Also it was supporting from its funds over fifteen hundred widows and persons in distress.[88] In addition to this multitude, "supported

[88] The yearly income necessary for support of the clergy and for these charities has been variously estimated as from thirty to fifty thousand dollars. The estimate is conjectural, but the cost of staple articles of food in the Roman world at that time is fairly well known and furnishes a basis for judgment, from which the suggested figures have been derived.

77

by the favor and philanthropy of the Master," there was also in the church a number of persons who were "through the providence of God rich and growing more prosperous."[39]

By the end of the third century the Christian religion was well along the way to economic success. Its membership included not a few well-to-do persons, a large body of wage-earners and moderately prosperous people who had been trained in habits of systematic giving, and a throng of needy individuals who subsisted mainly on Christian charity. The church itself had become a powerful financial institution with a regular income from the contributions of the members as well as from substantial property holdings that had come under its control. Among its officials were men of business experience and ability who not only increased the financial power of the institution, but at the same time were successful in business on their own account. When Christianity became officially tolerated by the state in the early fourth century much property confiscated in the Diocletian persecution had now to be restored. Constantine not only stressed this point in his instruction to his subordinates, but also recognized the administrative efficiency of the Christian institution by handing over funds for it to use. He thought the church at Carthage competent to receive and expend, for recouping religious conditions in that sec-

[39] Eusebius, *History*, VI. 43, quoting a letter of Cornelius, bishop of Rome, sent to Fabius of Antioch shortly after 250 A.D.

tion of the empire, a sum from the imperial treasury equivalent to perhaps one hundred thousand dollars.[40]

Under imperial patronage the financial prosperity of the church as an institution, and of its members as individuals, rapidly increased. Conditions at Antioch illustrate the situation at the close of the fourth century, when Christianity had been made the only legal religion of the empire. Chrysostom estimated that one-tenth of the members of the church at Antioch could properly be termed wealthy, another tenth was utterly poor, and the rest were moderately well-off. The total revenue of the church as an institution was less than the personal income of many of its rich members. Yet it supported from its regular budget three thousand widows and virgins, besides ministering to needy people who were in prison, in lodging-houses, out of work, strangers in the city, those who waited upon the altar, and others who came daily seeking food and clothing. Knowing the wealth that was at the disposal of individual Christians, Chrysostom lamented that a single person should have been in need. Poverty could be completely banished from the Christian community if the very rich and those in comfortable circumstances would show a little more interest in the welfare of humanity. Indeed, if they were to apportion

[40] According to Eusebius, *History*, X. 6. 1-3, Constantine, probably in 313 A.D., had instructed his finance minister of Africa to hand over to the bishop of Carthage three thousand "money bags" (*folles*), and had promised that the imperial treasurer would add to this sum if necessary. For the probable value of the *follis*, see the discussion on this word in Pauly-Wissowa, *op. cit.*, Vol. VI, cols. 2828-2838.

among themselves the persons needing food and clothing, Chrysostom estimates that not more than one poor man would fall to the care of a group of fifty or even a hundred affluent church members. If as few as ten men in the church would "sow with a full hand" there would be no poor person left.[41]

IV

The attention given to charity was the conspicuously redeeming feature in connection with Christianity's acquisition of worldly goods. Its aim from the outset had been to minister to the poor, and it steadfastly defended the right of the needy to share in the possessions of their more prosperous brethren. As a mutually helpful brotherhood, the church always maintained in spirit and practice the supremacy of the charitable ideal. The homeless were given shelter, the hungry were fed, the naked were clothed, hospitality was freely extended to visiting brethren, the sick and unfortunate were cared for, work was secured for the unemployed, and aid was made available for every form of need.[42]

Funds for the charitable works of the church were obtained from purely voluntary gifts; there was no form of institutional compulsion or regulation as to the amount of one's contribution. Christian teachers

[41] Chrysostom, *Homily,* lxvi. 3, on Matt. 20:29 f.

[42] Full statistics on these activities for the first three centuries may be found in A. Harnack, *Mission and Expansion of Christianity* (Second edition, New York, 1908), Vol. I, pages 147-198, the chapter on "The Gospel of Love and Charity."

took pains to stress the fact that the new religion could not be bought at any price in gold; it had no initiation fees and no stated monthly dues, like the contemporary guilds. The penniless were as welcome as the prosperous. Each convert was urged to contribute regularly to the church's treasure chest, the amount being determined entirely by the financial ability and disposition of the donor. The moral value of the act was safeguarded by rigid insistence upon the voluntary motive. Christianity aimed to soften men's hearts and inspire their generous impulses, but not to exercise mechanical lordship over their purses. Of communism in any strict sense of the word, either in theory or in practice, the ancient Christian society knew nothing. Members boasted that they had all things in common, while at the same time everyone's property was entirely subject to his own will. Christians liked to believe that their devotion to the ideals of the religious brotherhood was their fundamental and dominant motive.

Paul's advice to the Corinthians to set aside on a specific day money for charitable purposes[43] was the method followed in later years for obtaining funds to defray the expenses of the church. The Sunday service of the Roman congregation in the middle of the second century closed with the offering. Following the observance of the Eucharist, "each of those who are prosperous and so inclined gives voluntarily according to his own desire; then the amount collected is de-

[43] I Cor. 16:2.

posited with the president and he provides for the orphans and widows, for those who from sickness or any other cause are in want, for those who are in prison, for the strangers who tarry with us, and in brief he takes charge of all who are in need."[44] In Carthage the collection was taken monthly, when those members of the community who felt so disposed brought offerings made according to their ability—"no one is under compulsion, but his act is spontaneous." These "fruits of piety" were used "to feed and bury the poor, to succor boys and girls who have neither property nor parents,[45] to help aged domestics, and to relieve those who have been shipwrecked. If any are contending with affliction in the mines, or in banishment on the islands, or in prisons, simply on account of God's cause, they become the nurslings of the religion they have confessed."[46]

These simple processes inevitably grew more complicated in the course of time. Almsgiving, as a means of acquiring special merit in the sight of God, induced many persons to mingle this virtue with motives that sometimes seem to us more selfish than altruistic, but the result was no less significant for the financial resources of the church. Further attention was also given to providing an adequate machinery for the maintenance and expenditure of the growing income of the church. In other words, even charitable activities had to

[44] Justin, *Apology*, i. 67. 6.
[45] Cf. Roman "alimenta" mentioned above, p. 25.
[46] Tertullian, *Apology*, xxxix. 5 f.

82

be more extensively institutionalized in order to strengthen and extend the Christian service to society. Bishops, presbyters, deacons, and their assistants, serving a large Christian community, like that of Rome, Carthage, Alexandria, or Antioch, having an annual budget of several thousands of dollars, were compelled in the nature of the case to devise an efficient institutional administration. The primary responsibility rested with the bishop, whose ability as a business man was therefore of no slight importance for the welfare of Christianity. It is no accident that emperors who ultimately tolerated or espoused Christianity held in high esteem and drew into their counsels bishops like Cæcilianus of Carthage, Hosius of Cordova, Eusebius of Nicomedia, or Ambrose of Milan. As efficient and experienced men of affairs such bishops readily proved themselves the peers of even the most competent rulers.

The practice of Christian charity was not merely an individual affair; it operated on a world-scale and attracted wide attention even beyond the inner circle of the church. The welfare of each Christian group throughout the empire was close to the heart of every other church, especially of the larger communities in the great cities. The interest of the Pauline churches in the physical well-being of the church at Jerusalem, and the story of the aid sent by the church at Antioch to relieve the distress of their Palestinian brethren in a time of famine,[47] were examples emulated on a large scale in subsequent times. Local outbreaks of violence

[47] Acts 11:27-30.

83

against unfortunate Christian communities provided the opportunity for neighboring churches to perform a brotherly service by sending money to ransom prisoners, to minister to exiles in their distress, to help those who had lost their property, and to aid in the rehabilitation of the community's life. This distress was sometimes the result of persecution by the authorities and sometimes a consequence of barbarian incursions on the outskirts of the empire. In either case the church found therein a welcome opportunity to display its spirit of world-brotherhood, by which the financial resources of Christendom at large were made available for persons in distress on the remotest boundaries of the Roman world.

The Roman Church early gained an enviable reputation for its activity in world-wide service. Before the close of the second century its fame as a helper of needy Christian communities in distant regions had been firmly established. Apparently it always had in hand, or could immediately assemble, funds for these emergencies, and appreciation of its activities came from various quarters.[48] The church of Carthage followed the same custom, a notable instance of which was the sending of relief to the churches of Numidia in 253 A.D. The country had suddenly suffered from bandits who had carried away many Christian captives. Immediately the Carthaginian Church raised and dispatched the sum of 100,000 sesterces—some four

[48] *E.g.*, Dionysius of Corinth and Dionysius of Alexandria (Eusebius, *History*, IV. 23. 10 and VII. 5. 2) and Basil, *Letter* 70.

84

thousand dollars—to be used in ransoming the captives. Acts of this sort, rendered possible by Christianity's strong sense of common brotherhood and its rapidly developing financial ability, made it a recognized power in the social life of the day long before it had developed any specific institutional machinery to represent and administer its ecumenical interests.

The bishops of the individual churches were for many years the chief functionaries concerned with the collection and distribution of ecclesiastical funds. These officials, and all of the lesser clergy who served the church, drew, according to their needs, upon the money of the church for their support. They, too, administered help to widows, orphans, and all others in want. The individual church was a law unto itself in financial matters, but there was always a large measure of uniformity in practice answering to like necessities in the various communities. When the leader in any church deviated from custom, or showed himself negligent in maintaining the financial efficiency of his congregation, neighboring bishops at the larger centers like Rome, Carthage, Alexandria, or elsewhere, stood ready to offer brotherly advice or, if need be, to admonish and condemn. Synods gradually grew in importance, until under Constantine and his successors official councils assumed responsibility for unifying the practices and beliefs of Christendom. But already the economic procedure of the principal churches had become so thoroughly established that synods and councils merely undertook to confirm current practice or

85

to warn against abuses in the management of the funds of the local church.

Members of the clergy, especially bishops, presbyters, and deacons, had to be competent in business affairs if they were to render efficient service in the administration of so substantial a financial institution as the church had become by the close of the third century. As men of affairs, they were sometimes unavoidably subject to misunderstanding and criticism on the ground of failing to discriminate strictly between ecclesiastical and personal concerns. Cyprian, in the middle of the third century, had felt it necessary to condemn evidences of avarice among certain clerics, who seemed to him more eager to obtain advantageous markets and to collect interest on their investments, than to administer dutifully the activities of the church.[49] Clerics, even bishops, were frequently admonished by the decrees of synods and councils to subordinate admissible secular business to their duties as ecclesiastics.

Apparently members of the clergy often needed to be reminded that their first duty was to the church. It was universally conceded that those who "waited upon the altar" were fully entitled to support from the common fund of the religious community, but they were urged to draw upon this source only when their private income was insufficient, and then only for the bare necessities of the simplest kind of life.[50] Fol-

[49] Cyprian, *On the Lapsed*, 6.
[50] *Didascalia*, viii.

86

lowing the apostolic example, they were to be content with simple food and plain clothing. Capable clerics undoubtedly felt in duty bound to use their business ability not only to insure support for themselves and their families, but to acquire income from which a contribution could be made to the funds of the church.

The conduct of secular business by members of the clergy was regarded not only as a privilege but as a duty of church officials during the early centuries of Christian history, provided their religious activities were not thereby neglected. They were encouraged to work at various handicrafts during their spare hours, in order that they, along with all the brethren, might be productive agents within the church.[51] When they were capable of engaging in successful business activities their earning power was augmented without lessening the time left at their disposal for the service of religion. The earliest intimation of an effort to restrict their commercial operations appears about the year 300, when the Synod of Elvira ruled[52] that bishops, presbyters, and deacons must not leave their own community to hunt profitable markets elsewhere. This procedure would, naturally, result in temporary neglect of the local church. But no judgment was pronounced against the pursuit of secular business in the place of their residence, and it was distinctly stated that they might properly delegate a son, a freedman,

[51] See W. Bright, *Canons of the First Four General Councils* (Second edition, Oxford, 1892), pp. 156 f.
[52] *Canon*, xix.

87

a paid agent, or a friend to represent their interests in other regions. Secular business under the control of clergymen was, as such, assumed to be entirely legitimate.

In later times the need for more rigid restrictions came to be keenly felt. Various dangers were involved. The dissipation of time and energy that ought to be devoted to the church was not the only menace to be feared. There was also the temptation to avarice, the possibility that unfavorable criticism might be incurred by Christianity, and a danger lest clerics might use for private ends the funds of the church. Letting out money or property at interest was one of the most serious problems. The legal rate of interest in the Roman Empire until the time of Justinian was twelve per cent, and Christian men in business accepted the custom in spite of the Old Testament prohibition of usury.[53] In acting thus, probably they felt no greater impropriety than they did in setting aside the Mosaic injunction against shaving the beard. Moreover, they read in the New Testament Jesus' criticism of the man who had failed to place his money with the bankers, thus preventing Jesus from receiving his own "with usury."[54]

Nevertheless, the authorities of the church finally decided that, so far at least as the clergy were concerned, the taking of usury should be suppressed. It lent itself too readily to "covetousness and lust for gain," as the

[53] *E.g.,* Ps. 15:5, and many other passages.
[54] Matt. 25:27; Luke 19:23.

88

danger was phrased in the legislation of the Nicene Council in 325 A.D.[55] Not only the customary twelve per cent was disallowed, but any other similar device, such as receiving the original loan and "one half in kind," or "any other scheme whatsoever for the sake of filthy lucre" was pronounced henceforth improper and was to be punished by dismissing the transgressor from office and erasing his name from the clerical list. But evidently the practice had become so thoroughly established in the business activities of the clergy that it could not be easily eliminated, and future synods and councils found it necessary to issue further condemnatory legislation on the subject.[56]

Unquestionably the church had profited immensely by calling into its service as leaders some of the most capable business men of the Roman world. At the same time its moral and spiritual ideals had to be safeguarded by raising barriers against the dangers of secularization and questionable business practices. The menace was a real one, but the church as a whole stoutly maintained the supremacy of its religious aims. Prosperity was made to serve Christianity, although some Christians even among the clergy yielded to the blandishments of wealth. Bishops and deacons were warned against receiving "tainted" money, even when it could be used effectively to feed and clothe the poor.

[55] *Canon*, xvii; cf. *Canons of Elvira*, xx; *Canons of Arles*, xii.

[56] *E.g.*, *Canons of Laodicea*, iv; *Apostolic Canons*, xliv; Basil, *Letter* 188. 14. Note the special tortures provided for usurers taking compound interest, in the *Apocalypse of Peter* (Akhmim fragment, 31); also Cyprian, *On the Lapsed*, 6; Eusebius, *History*, V. 18. 11.

89

The church must not sell itself to the world for gold by receiving gifts from the unworthy who hoped to benefit in return from the Christian prayers of the needy recipients.[57]

It was felt necessary also to warn the bishop against laying himself open to the charge of mismanaging or misappropriating ecclesiastical funds. Members of his own immediate family were not to be given a privileged position in the financial business of the church, but a properly constituted supervisory committee of responsible persons should be set up to help in the management. And great care had to be exercised in avoiding any confusion between the property or money belonging to the church and that possessed personally by the bishop.[58] The temptation to simony was also not unknown even in the ancient church, but it was severely condemned;[59] as was the disposition of some bishops to remove from their original sees when a more lucrative or otherwise more desirable bishopric elsewhere could be obtained by negotiations.[60] And some bishops were not averse to holding more than one see, so that "pluralities" had also to be rigorously forbidden.[61]

The definitive position of the church with respect to the clergy in business was finally enunciated in de-

[57] *Didascalia,* xviii.

[58] *Canons of Antioch,* xxv; *Canons of Chalcedon,* xxii; *Apostolic Canons,* xxxviii-xli.

[59] *Canons of Nicea,* xv f.; *Canons of Chalcedon,* ii.

[60] *Canons of Constantinople,* ii.

[61] *Canons of Chalcedon,* x.

90

tail at the Council of Chalcedon in 451 A.D. Discredit had been brought upon Christianity by the unworthy actions of some persons holding clerical positions that were being used for personal profit. These individuals sought to become managers of other people's property, or ingratiated themselves in the houses of the wealthy whose possession they coveted. Therefore "the holy and great council has decreed that in future no bishop or clergyman or monk shall either lease possessions, or engage in business, or occupy himself with the management of worldly goods, except he shall be required by the law to assume the guardianship of minors; or the bishop of his city shall commit to him, for the fear of God, the care of ecclesiastical affairs, or of orphans or improvident widows and of persons who are particularly in need of the aid of the church. And if in future anyone shall violate these ordinances he shall be punished with ecclesiastical penalties."[62] The clergy were not to suppress their business ability but were to devote their skill and energy wholly to the concerns of the church.

In the course of three centuries the original indifference of Christians toward worldly goods had been completely supplanted by a determination on the part of the church to bring the material resources of the world into the service of religion. This effort was transfused by the Christian ideal of brotherhood and glorified by the devotion of the Christian communities to charitable activities. The altruistic motive had been fundamental

[62] *Canon,* iii.

91

in launching the church as an institution upon its persistent quest for worldly goods, a goal that could be attained only as adherents of the new religion themselves became prosperous people. While worldly concerns were always held to be of secondary importance, and relatively worthless in comparison with the treasures of heaven, the city of God on earth needed for its temporal structure the materials of the physical world which the good God had himself created for the use of his servants on earth.

Three centuries of struggle had brought Christianity to a position of prominence in the economic life of the Roman world. Even pagans who ridiculed the ease with which impostors could live on Christian charity, could not fail to be impressed by its magnificence. Let one of their number find himself in peril, and Christians from all the neighboring communities became at once alert, ungrudgingly forwarding large sums of money to aid those in distress.[63] And when Julian endeavored to rehabilitate the heathen cults in the latter part of the fourth century, he could think of no higher ideal of economic efficiency to be emulated by their priests than the practice of the "impious Galileans" who "nourish both their own needy and ours also."[64] No testimony to Christianity's material efficiency could have spoken in more convincing terms to that ancient world than did its superabundant charitable activities.

[63] So it seemed to the pagan satirist, Lucian, when near the beginning of the third century he wrote his *Peregrinus,* 11-16.

[64] *Letters,* 49.

92

Largely as a result of its attainment of economic prestige the new religion was able to forsake the rough and dusty bypaths which formerly it had been forced to pursue and could now boldly emerge a dignified traveler upon the main highway to social respectability.

III. *Christianity and Social Prestige*

III

Christianity and Social Prestige

WHEN CHRISTIANITY FIRST ATTRACTED PUBLIC NOTICE IN the Roman Empire the people who accounted themselves most respectable shunned the new religion. They regarded its followers with indifference, if not with disdain. Its prophetic forerunner had been a roughly clad anchorite preaching in the Judean desert, its founder had been an unschooled artisan from a small Galilean village, his most prominent disciples in Palestine were "unlearned and ignorant" fishermen, and his first ardent advocate among the Gentiles was a migratory Jewish tentmaker who early gained notoriety with the authorities as a disturber of the peace. Christians were people who "turned the world upside down." That a religion so utterly lacking in social prestige at the outset, should ultimately become the only respectable faith for men of culture and high position in the Roman Empire, is one of the most astounding facts in ancient history.

I

Not least among the obstacles to be overcome by the new religion was the state of mind of its own leaders. At first they had no desire to attain social prestige. They declared the present status of mankind to be an evil form of existence destined to be overthrown by a sudden and violent intervention of their God. All power, dignity, privilege, and culture, that marked the contemporary civilization, would be quickly swept aside with the return of Christ at an early date to inaugurate the kingdom of God. The end was so near that converts were advised to seize the new age in advance by living now as though it had already arrived. "Brethren, the time has grown shorter. In the period that remains let those that have wives be as those that have none, and those that mourn as those that do not, and those that rejoice as those that do not, and those that trade as those who possess nothing, and those acquiring worldly goods as those who have no property; for the present order of the world is on the point of passing away. I wish you to be free from anxieties."[1] The current social order was so hopelessly inadequate to mediate the worthiest values in life, and was so completely dominated by Satanic powers, that its absolute destruction was conceived to be the only condition on which the Christian ideal for mankind was capable of realization.

As the years wore on, the hope of Christ's return had to be pushed farther and farther into the future. Yet the expectation was not abandoned, nor did Christians readily surrender their pessimistic interpretation of contemporary society. They did not neglect to emulate the apostolic ideal of accommodating their message to the capacities of their hearers, to the end that

[1] I Cor. 7:29-32.

98

"certain ones" should be saved,[2] but they stoutly maintained the impossibility of making the Christian Gospel permanently at home in the present world. "This age" was destined, not for salvation, but for destruction; it had to perish in order to clear the stage for the incoming "new age" when those who now believed would finally enter into the full realization of their salvation. As yet they could not imagine that the present complex social order could be effectively christianized by a gradual process of evangelization. On the contrary, the task of Christianity was to make haste in rescuing individuals from a doomed society trembling on the verge of collapse. Relative to the total population of the Roman Empire, they were few who would be privileged to enter the gates of the New Jerusalem. The pathway thither was narrow and traveled by a small number, in comparison with the multitudes that thronged the broad road to destruction.[3]

Throughout the second century leading Christian spokesmen continued to allege the worthlessness of the present age in comparison with the new age to be inaugurated by Christ. Even though its establishment might lie in the far distant future, pious imagination made it a vivid reality for Christians at the present moment. They were to live as if it were imminent, an expectation long cherished especially by the more zealous chiliasts. Considerations of time were relatively unessential. With the Lord one day might be as a

[2] I Cor. 9:22.
[3] Matt. 7:13 f.; Luke 13:23 f.

99

thousand years and a thousand years as one day. Ultimately a new heaven and a new earth would be set up wherein righteousness would find its perfect manifestation. Postponement of the end could be easily explained. It was a generous provision of God to allow mankind a longer period for repentance; or it was in accordance with the divine scheme for entrapping the demons, while the church assembled the predestined number of the saints who were to be citizens in the new regime.[4]

Those who thus lived, with their gaze riveted upon the ideal society to be realized in the coming age, were incapable of highly appreciating the worth of life in the present. They were mere sojourners in this sinful environment, while their true citizenship was in the new society still awaiting its establishment. The immediate task of the church was to rescue the few willing to forsake the ways of this evil age; it was no part of Christianity's duty to infuse the contemporary social life with the spirit of the new religion, or to shoulder upon its representatives the obligation to create a better world here and now for the benefit of mankind at large. The best Christian would endure afflictions without complaint in his self-sacrificing efforts to rescue needy mortals from thraldom in the world, but hope for humanity as a whole lay in the final overthrow of the present social order.

Christians of this temper ardently preached and devoutly practiced love for humanity, yet they hated and

[4] II Peter 3:1-13; Justin, *Apology*, I. 45. 1.

100

openly condemned Roman society. They failed to perceive the possibility of distinguishing between the evils in the life about them and the social structure in which these evils found embodiment. Since the two things were for them inseparable, the elimination of wickedness could be accomplished only by a violent act of God. While this temper prevailed it would have seemed a degradation to Christians had they acquired social respectability in the Roman Empire; it was of the very essence of Christianity that it should be an exotic phenomenon in a social order whose form and genius were irretrievably Satanic. A state of affairs displeasing to God was of necessity anathema to Christians, and they did not scruple to let it be known that in their heart of hearts they were the implacable foes of the demonic order to which their heathen contemporaries were devoting life and energy.

Almost two centuries passed before leading Christians came to realize that the task of the new religion was not simply to rescue a few saved persons from the menace of impending doom. Only slowly, and at first almost unconsciously, Christianity perceived that it was faced by the far more comprehensive task of rehabilitating the existing order through the tedious and often precarious process of living the Christian life in all the varied relationships of society. The present world was not to be wiped out suddenly by divine intervention; if the new religion was to triumph it must learn how, in the person of its adherents, to permeate the social structure and demonstrate the practicability of Christianity as a religion suitable to the continuing conditions of life in the Roman Empire.

This was not an easy lesson to learn. While the deprecatory estimate of heathen society, so stoutly proclaimed by the earliest Christian preachers, remained influential, acceptance of the gentile world as a permanent setting in which the Christian religion was to run its course normally from generation to generation could not be contemplated with any measure of satisfaction. Granting that God permitted the present social order to endure, one still felt constrained to pursue a consistent policy of aloofness. Christian purity could be maintained only by keeping oneself unspotted from the world.[5] Christians were desirous of having the world think well of them, but were unwilling to alter their judgment as to its utterly evil character. Teachers and preachers constantly emphasized the importance of so living as to give no offence to the heathen, but Christians were no less strenuously warned against the danger of incurring God's displeasure by associating too freely with their non-Christian neighbors in the ordinary affairs of daily life.

Christian hostility to heathen society was answered by a not unnatural disdain for Christianity on the part of the Roman world. Herein was another serious obstacle to Christianity's attainment of social prestige in its ancient environment. In the first place, it suffered the handicap of its Jewish ancestry. During the century preceding the rise of Christianity Jews had spread

[5] Jas. 1:27; 4:4.

102

themselves widely around the Mediterranean basin, where they enjoyed a recognized position in society. Under Julius Cæsar and Augustus they had been granted many favors, but under subsequent emperors their social position somewhat deteriorated.[6] Their refusal to participate heartily in the life of the heathen world, a necessary counterpart to their exclusiveness in religion, marked them as an exotic element in the population. Moreover, the rebellious conduct of their kinsmen in Palestine during the first and early second centuries A.D. further augmented the popular hatred and disgust with which they were regarded by the upper classes in the Roman Empire.

Jews were conspicuous in that flood of Oriental immigrants pouring into Rome, like the emptying of the Syrian Orontes into the pure waters of the Tiber.[7] The Eternal City was becoming a cesspool that received the dregs of the world.[8] The Roman aristocrat could not view with complacence this adulteration of the population. When, under Tiberius, the Senate took action to suppress the religious rites of "Jews and Egyptians," and four thousand freedmen infected with this superstition were deported to Sardinia to check banditry in the island, the Roman officials were gratified with the prospect that the unhealthful climate would prove fatal to those forced into this service. This outcome would

[6] The status of the Jews in the Roman Empire has been most fully studied by J. Juster, *Les Juifs dans l'empire romain. Leur condition juridique, économique et sociale.* 2 vols. (Paris, 1914).

[7] Juvenal, *Satire,* III. 60-65.

[8] Tacitus, *Annals,* XV. 44.

103

be of "no great consequence," and those not thus drafted were required to leave Italy unless by an appointed time they "renounced their impious rites."[9] Orientals, and Jews in particular, were the objects of much popular hatred at Rome, and violent outbreaks against them often occurred. Christianity naturally suffered from this prejudice. It, too, had arisen in Judea, and when first it attracted public attention it seemed to the authorities to be simply a new Jewish sect.[10]

When the distinction between Christianity and Judaism was more sharply drawn by critics, the result was not especially to the advantage of Christianity. In fact, Christians had so emphatically repudiated the Jews that the new religion gladly sacrificed any measure of social recognition which might have accrued to membership in the Jewish community. Socially, the breach between Jews and Christians was often wider than that between Christians and heathens. Thus Christianity sank to a third level of esteem in the eyes of its gentile enemies. It was not only lower than heathenism, but lower even than Judaism. Christians were at best said to be only renegade Jews, who rudely severed themselves from society, whether Jewish or gentile. They were called persons "who cut themselves off and break away from the rest of mankind."[11] Furthermore,

[9] Tacitus, *Annals*, II. 85; Suetonius, *Tiberius*, 36; Josephus, *Antiquities*, XVIII. 3. 5.

[10] This confusion of thought appears to have been in the mind of Suetonius when he remarked that Claudius banished the Jews from Rome because of the riots instigated by one called Chrestus.—*Claudius*, 25.

[11] Origen, *Celsus*, VIII. 2.

104

they did not pay reverence in the current way to the Deity worshiped by the Jews, but fashioned for themselves a certain impossible mode of life, new and solitary, and not in accord with the customs of either Greeks or Jews."[12]

From the gentile point of view, Christianity, like Judaism, was both exclusive and non-social. Apparently this was the common belief of Roman writers and officials in the second century. Christians themselves could hardly have disputed this opinion, although they would have resented the inferences drawn therefrom and the terms used to describe their attitude. They did not aspire to be unpopular with their neighbors, but their unyielding attitude toward the characteristic activities of heathen society, and their doctrine of its early destruction, invited unfavorable comment. How a Gentile, who knew Christianity only from its exterior aspect, could have thought Christians to be other than an undesirable and even despicable element in the population is difficult to imagine. It was a perfectly normal state of affairs that made them so generally hated at Rome in Nero's day as to be likely scapegoats on whom he might saddle the blame for the great fire of 64 A.D.

If one visualizes concretely the daily conduct of a Christian emulating the ideals of his more rigorous teachers in the early decades of gentile Christianity's history, the deprecatory judgments of the heathen will

---

[12] Probably the criticism of Porphyry is here reflected by Eusebius, *Preparation for the Gospel*, I. 2.

105

not be surprising. On accepting the new religion the convert immediately ceased to purchase images and garlands to decorate his home on festive occasions. He no longer participated in the characteristic religious activities of the heathen. He offered no sacrifices at the temples, he contributed no money to their treasuries, and he absented himself from the holiday ceremonies in which his neighbors found joy and pride. He soon became known as an undesirable person who refused to bear his share in maintaining those activities thought essential to the life of every self-respecting civic community.

Roman writers who referred slightingly to Christianity were fully as generous as could have been expected under the circumstances. Christians, by their non-social attitudes, readily incurred the charge of being "haters of the human race."[13] The poor man who had joined their group, thereby experiencing its generosity and love of the brethren, knew that this harsh accusation was false, but it could not be expected that aristocratic outsiders would share this appreciative estimate of the new religion. Moreover, to the Roman mind all worthy religion was public in character and welcomed the full light of day upon its ceremonies. Suspicion attached to any cult that performed its sacred rites behind closed doors. Ceremonies like the Christian eucharist, to which only the initiated were admitted, could, in traditional Roman thinking, have no other motive for secrecy than that of veiling from the public

[13] Tacitus, *Annals*, XV. 44.

gaze some improper performance. It seemed very likely that Christians at such times practiced "enormities," and this smoldering suspicion was quickly fanned into flame by irresponsible gossip about eating flesh and drinking blood and practicing promiscuous osculation. When an official took pains to investigate the conduct of Christians in their assemblies he might exonerate them from popular calumnies, and yet they seemed devoted to a "perverse and excessive superstition."[14]

II

Christian aloofness toward its heathen neighbors, and popular gentile belief that Christianity was inimical to the social order, were not the only serious difficulties in the way of the new religion's attaining respectability. Still another hindrance, hardly less formidable, was the fact that gentile Christianity drew a large majority of its converts from among the lower classes—slaves, ordinary manual laborers, common craftsmen, small shopkeepers, wandering artisans or peddlers, and the like. The proletarian character of the church's membership was readily admitted by Christian preachers, who, like Paul, rejoiced that God had not chosen to establish the true religion on any foundations of human knowledge, power, or social dignity.[15] Rather, God in his infinite wisdom had se-

[14] Pliny, *Epistles*, X. 96; Suetonius, *Nero*, 16. See further data on the popular accusations against Christians given below, pages 171 ff.
[15] I Cor. 1:26-29.

107

lected his followers from the lower and despised classes, in order that the church might not be tempted to pride itself on a worldly dignity measured by common human standards.

Class feeling was very strong in that ancient world. The way in which people were accustomed to earn a livelihood furnished the chief grounds on which social distinctions were estimated. Among both Greeks and Romans, agriculture as conducted by the gentleman farmer was a highly respected calling, while the characteristic activities of the ordinary man in the urban community, whether in manual labor or in trade, were rated on a relatively low plane. And Christianity, which was distinctly an urban rather than a rural movement, suffered the disadvantages of its situation. Paul might boast that his gospel embodied a divine wisdom revealed to the ignorant proletariat, but to the cultured Greek or aristocratic Roman, Christianity seemed to be a detestable superstition that tended to flourish among the lowest classes in the slums of the great cities. The social dignity of this religion corresponded, therefore, with the status occupied by such people, according to the standards of judgment then in vogue.

These standards were well known and widely accepted, but were so very different from those of modern times that one needs to give them special notice in order to comprehend the actual situation confronted by Christianity. The question of what callings were honorable and what dishonorable was often discussed

108

in ancient literature. The Romans from an early date had developed a definite tradition on the subject, to which writers in the early imperial age frequently recurred.[16] In the third century B.C. Cato, in his work on agriculture, had idealized life on the farm. Commerce was not inherently bad, but was liable to many risks and so should be avoided. Banking, if honestly conducted, was not to be disdained, but one who took usury was worse than a thief. Also the practice of medicine was to be spurned. The first Roman doctors came mostly from Greece and were, in Cato's opinion, chiefly bent on poisoning the Romans. Philosophers, who in the early period of their activity at Rome also came from Greece, were looked upon with suspicion, and were forcibly suppressed on more than one occasion. As late as the time of Nero another Roman admirer of agriculture, Columella, also denounced lawyers, who were, he said, engaged in "dog-business," since their specialty was barking at the rich.

It was Cicero who at the close of the Republic composed on this subject, as on so many other themes, the statement that became the norm for subsequent Roman opinion. Regarding occupations and pursuits worthy of honor we accept, wrote Cicero, approximately the following: "First, those pursuits which incur men's displeasure, such as the collecting of customs and the loaning of money at interest, are disapproved. Ignoble

[16] The Roman literature on this theme has been studied in detail by W. E. Heitland, *Agricola: A Study of Agriculture and Rustic Life in the Græco-Roman World from the Point of View of Labor.* (Cambridge, 1921.)

and unworthy also are the trades of all hired laborers, and of all who are paid for their toil rather than their skill. For in their case it is the remuneration itself for which they work. Those also who purchase for immediate sale goods from wholesale dealers must be considered unworthy, for they obtain no profit unless they are huge liars. Indeed, nothing is more disgraceful than falsehood. And all mechanics are engaged in an unworthy occupation, for nothing worthy of a freeman can be had in a workshop. Least of all are those pursuits to be approved which minister to pleasures, as Terence says, fishmongers, butchers, cooks, sausage-makers, fishermen. One may add also dealers in perfume, dancers, and everything connected with the game of dice. But those occupations for which greater intelligence is required, or from which exceptional usefulness is derived, like medicine, architecture, and education, are honorable for those whose social rank is suited to the calling. Trade, if conducted on a small scale, must be adjudged unworthy, but if it is a big and profitable business importing many commodities from every quarter of the earth and shared in by many persons without deceit, is not to be utterly disparaged." These big merchants could redeem themselves by investing their profits in land upon which they retired as gentleman farmers, "for of all profitable employments, nothing is better than agriculture, nothing more productive, nothing more agreeable, nothing more worthy of a free man."[17]

[17] Cicero, *Offices*, I. 42.

When one recalls the range of occupations in which Christians were to be found earning a livelihood and acquiring economic stability in the Roman Empire,[18] it becomes perfectly apparent that they could never have attained to social respectability had the Ciceronian standard of judgment prevailed. Undoubtedly Christians themselves did much during the first three centuries of their history to alter traditional opinions on this subject. But they were not fighting the battle alone. Heathen philosophers and educators were also attempting a reformation of popular opinion, from the results of which Christianity profited. Men of Seneca's kindly disposition ventured temperate criticisms by remarking that one may be able to discharge one's duty to the common laborer by paying him his price, but to the artist or skilled workman we still owe a debt of respect which cannot be fully discharged by the payment of any stated wage, while in the case of the physician or teacher there is also a debt due that cannot be paid in terms of any fee.[19] Bolder Stoic philosophers, like Epictetus, were more insistent on the inherent dignity of all labor, even that of a slave. They maintained that it had been no disgrace for a philosopher like Socrates to toil to support his family—even a wife like Xantippe —or for the famous Cleanthes to work as a water-carrier all day in order to acquire the means with which to carry on his philosophical studies at night.[20]

[18] See above, pages 56-70.
[19] Seneca, *Benefits*, VI. 17.
[20] Epictetus, *Discourses*, III. 26. I; Basil, *Letter* 4.

Among the growing number of heathen preachers who defended the social respectability of the poor man and the common laborer, Dio Chrysostom is especially deserving of note. He was one of those educated public lecturers who had been born of prosperous parents in the East, but later chose the life of hardship that characterized the Stoic missionary of that age. In the second decade of the second century, when Christians were beginning their struggle for greater recognition in society, he delivered a lecture, apparently at Rome, in which he dealt very candidly with the conditions of life led by the poor working people in the cities of the Roman Empire.[21] His main contention was that poverty, instead of constituting a handicap, really gave one an advantage over the rich man when it came to living a seemly and natural life fruitful in words and deeds and social intercourse.

In respect to generosity, for example, Dio affirmed that it was in the home of the poor man that one would find the readiest display of hospitality. He was the quickest to kindle a fire to warm the stranger, the most ready to share his clothing with the shipwrecked mariner, and the most willing to go out of his way to direct a traveler on the road. The rich man was generous to those from whom he expected to receive a similar or greater favor, and his pretended acts of kindness turned out to be only a species of shrewd investment on which he expected to realize a high rate of interest. Apart from a few noble exceptions, the

[21] *Discourse* VII. 81-152.

112

generosity of the rich was at heart only a respectable parsimony, while the kindness shown by the poor man was an exhibition of unselfish and noble character. His charity did not express itself in costly gifts of silver goblets, embroidered garments or four-horse chariots, but in the common necessities of life, which by his own industry he could replace without thought of remuneration from the recipient. Thus poor people willing to work with their own hands were really more fortunately circumstanced in life than were those addicted to wealth and luxury.

Poverty, even among those who lived in the cities, was not to be deplored as essentially evil, nor was the common laborer to be regarded as an inferior member of society. On the contrary, his was quite as worthy a life as that of the banker busy with levying exorbitant rates of interest and calculating the times for collecting his revenues, or the landlord gathering his rents, or the merchant thinking of his ships and of the multitude of men in his service. While free from the anxieties and temptations that beset the rich, the poor man in the city might find himself in very narrow circumstances and unable to survive without charitable assistance. If he were in the country he would be more fortunate, but in the city everything had to be bought. Not even a few stray sticks for a fire could be had without money; water alone was free. But the respectability of the poor man was not lessened even though his only possession was his physical body and his only source of income the labor of his hands. Notwithstanding great poverty, such people were more desirable citizens than were many of the lazy well-to-do who plundered public funds and debased civic morals.

The test of noble living, stressed by Stoic and Christian preacher alike, was honest industry in honorable employments. The heathen moralist, Dio Chrysostom, like the Christian Clement of Alexandria three generations later, would have the common toiler feel the full dignity of worthy manhood and set aside the false standards of his critics by demonstrating in actual conduct his right to respect. Dio advised men to rise above those sneers that were often uttered against one's poverty or the lowliness of one's occupation. The good man was superior to these shallow prejudices. Let him see to it that he did not debase himself and his powers by pursuing unworthy employments, such as were connected with the dyeing, perfuming, and dressing of the hair of men and women, or the use of unguents and chemicals by which people attempted to counterfeit youthfulness or give a spurious appearance to one's person. One should also avoid those occupations followed by tragic and comic actors who spent their lives to no higher purpose than ministering to the passing pleasures and luxuries of mankind. Employments that contributed only to the shamelessness, pride, and arrogance of people were to be sedulously spurned.

Everything that tended to impair character was to be avoided. All activities connected with the thriving business of the brothels were scathingly condemned by

Dio. But there were other forms of employment, less openly vicious, that also catered to vulgarity and were debasing in spite of their popularity and success. Much of the public service at that time was classed as despicable. Such was the work of the clever informer, or of the conscienceless lawyer who sold himself for a fee irrespective of the virtue of the cause he defended. Let the poor not despise the humblest forms of honest handicraft, but there is no need that they become "tongue-craftsmen and law-craftsmen." On the other hand, let integrity be their true dignity, and let them regard every occupation as socially respectable that affords an opportunity to make an honest livelihood with their hands without involving one in immoral conduct or contributing in any manner to the injury of one's fellows.

The standards for measuring social respectability were already undergoing a gradual change even outside of Christian circles. The circumstance of life, especially in the urban communities, gave a new importance to strength of character, power of individual initiative, and competence in skilled workmanship. The man who was honest, industrious, and capable was found so necessary to the maintenance of life's affairs that he could command a certain type of social dignity regardless of his economic status or occupation. Both Stoic and Christian preachers, by making character the supreme test of social respectability, swept aside as false and unworthy many older notions. But it required a more powerful influence than mere preaching—whether Stoic or Christian—to effect completely so radical a transformation of traditional ideas as to admit the ordinary artisan or unskilled laborer to a position of recognized social dignity. This result was not accomplished primarily through the promulgation of a new social philosophy. Rather, a type of conduct was cultivated by toilers, especially by those who belonged to the fellowship of the church, that made itself practically effective over a wide area of interests. In the course of time Christians learned to think better of the world in which they were living, and it in turn found the presence of Christians more acceptable. But representatives of these divergent attitudes had to live through a multitude of concrete situations before their distrust of one another could be dissipated.

III

Notwithstanding the stress on aloofness in the social philosophy of Christian teachers, the rank and file of Christendom lived in intimate contact with their heathen neighbors. Under these circumstances the social status of the new religion was ultimately determined less by the idealism of its leaders than by the specific mode of life exemplified by the increasing body of its adherents. The key to the situation was in the hands of the convert who remained a member of the home and of the civic community in daily intercourse with non-Christian relatives and neighbors. The Christian way of life was on trial in all the varied relationships of the family, as well as in the wider social contacts of the city and the state.

At the outset a converted slave in a heathen household must have been socially a liability rather than an asset for Christianity. While Roman custom granted a large measure of religious freedom to slaves, their position religiously, like their status socially, was a distinctly inferior one.[22] Yet the church opened its doors freely to members of the slave class and allowed them positions of rank in the cult. They were granted all the privileges of the brotherhood and were esteemed as highly as any other member of the Christian community. Slaves who suffered in times of persecution became revered martyrs, and others rose to the first place among the clergy. The social stigma that Christianity thus acquired could not be easily shaken off, nor did the church seriously attempt to alter the situation. As a matter of fact, even Christianity, with all its emphasis on common human brotherhood, exerted relatively slight influence upon the popular attitude toward slavery. It carried on no propaganda aiming to elevate the social position of the slave in Roman society, nor did it advocate the abolition of the institution.

At least one step upward on the social ladder could have been taken by the church had it instituted a

[22] E.g., when the emperor Claudius, acting as high priest, celebrated special religious rites for the people, he first commanded that all common laborers and slaves should withdraw (Suetonius, *Claudius*, 22). Yet the religious rights of slaves were distinctly recognized. In summarizing the laws relating to Roman worship, Cicero had said that all work should cease on sacred days, so that even slaves would be able to take part in religious ceremonies (*Laws*, II. 8).

117

regular procedure for securing the manumission of converted slaves. They would then have acquired the status of freedmen. As early as the first quarter of the second century there appears to have been a desire on the part of some Christian slaves to have the church provide funds for the purchase of their liberty, evidently with a view to the attainment of a higher social position. But Christian leaders frowned upon this ambition. On one occasion the bishop of Antioch in Syria wrote to his fellow bishop in Smyrna: "Do not scorn slaves, male and female, yet let them not be puffed up but let them render full service unto the glory of God in order that they may obtain from God a better freedom. Let them not yearn to have their liberty purchased with money from the common fund, lest they be found slaves of desire."[23]

The leaders of the church made no effort to advance the social respectability of itself as a group, or of its slave members, by abolishing the slave class. The prevailing disposition of Christianity was opposed to any move in this direction. Kindness in the treatment of slaves was inculcated with diligence, but the abolition of the institution, even among Christians themselves, was not encouraged. In the event that a Christian slave was subject to harsh treatment by a heathen master, the feeling of brotherhood inspired some heroic efforts to secure his freedom. Christian freemen were known to have sold themselves into slavery in order to obtain money to liberate others

[23] Ignatius, *Polycarp* 4.

118

more unfortunately situated,[24] and for a Christian master to manumit his slaves was always a praiseworthy act, but it was by no means an established duty. Slaves in the Christian household were admonished to obey their masters in humility and respect, even as they obeyed God himself.[25] And any general effort to obtain freedom from heathen masters was consistently discouraged. The church did not seek social advancement through the liberation of its slave membership. It was content to leave them in their present status to exemplify as individuals in their personal living the moral ideals of Christianity, while the new religion attained a higher social standing by adding to its membership converts from the higher classes of society. In time this became a more conscious effort on the part of the church, and resulted in a corresponding tendency within the Christian community to treat slaves as a socially inferior class.

Within the inner circle of the family, the acceptance of Christianity by only one member of the group could not fail to produce a measure of social embarrassment. If a wife or a daughter or a husband or a son alone joined the new religion, the other members of the family naturally felt that their social standing among their heathen friends had been in a measure lowered. When the entire household allied itself with the church the conditions in the home could be conveniently adjusted to the new way of living, but the

[24] I Clement, lv. 2: *Didascalia* xvii.
[25] *Didache* iv. 12.

119

relations of the family to non-Christian acquaintances in the community still presented serious problems. A business or professional man lost caste with his customers and clients as soon as they learned that he had joined the unpopular Christian cult, and his acquaintances in the church were not sufficiently numerous to supply a new circle of patrons capable of replacing those who had been alienated by his change of religious affiliations. Under such circumstances the problem of pursuing the Christian way of life without forfeiting the respect of heathen neighbors presented a situation that must have occasioned no little anxiety and inconvenience for many persons in the early church.

Christianity, like Judaism, proved especially attractive to women in the Roman Empire. They were prominent in the activities of the church.[26] This fact, already evident in New Testament times, continued to be a characteristic feature of the Christian religion for cen-

[26] Note the statistical summary on this topic in A. Harnack, *Mission and Expansion of Christianity*, Vol. II, pages 64-84; also Elfriede Gottlieb, *Die Frau im frühen Christentum* (Leipzig, 1928); H. Preisker, *Christentum und Ehe in den ersten drei Jahrhunderten* (Berlin, 1927); J. Köhne, *Die Ehe zwischen Christen und Heiden in den ersten christlichen Jahrhunderten* (Paderborn, 1931); W. Braun, *Die Frau in die alten Kirche* (Berlin, 1919); J. P. Kirsch, *Die Frauen des kirchlichen Altertums* (Paderborn, 1912); E. von der Goltz, *Der Dienst der Frau in der christlichen Kirche*, 2 vols., Second Edition (Potsdam, 1914); Lydia Stöcker, *Die Frau in die alten Kirche* (Tübingen, 1907); L. Zscharnack, *Der Dienst der Frau in den ersten Jahrhunderten der christlichen Kirche* (Göttingen, 1902); Henriette Dacier, *Saint Jean Chrysostome et la femme chrétienne au IVe siècle de l'église grecque* (Paris, 1907); J. Donaldson, *Woman, Her Position in Ancient Greece and Rome and among the Early Christians* (London, 1907); T. B. Allworthy, *Women in the Apostolic Church* (Cambridge, 1917).

120

turies. Yet the situation of the Christian woman in relation to her kinsfolk and neighbors was often a difficult one.[27] If her husband were a heathen, or if she were an unmarried daughter of non-Christian parents, her social position was seriously imperiled by membership in a religion that was frowned upon by the rest of the household, as well as by the majority of her acquaintances in the heathen community. Her old friends often regarded her, either openly or secretly, as a social outcast.

Christian "widows" and "virgins"—the latter especially in the East—early became distinctly recognized groups in the church, which made definite provisions for their support. Thus they were relieved of the difficulties of living the Christian life in the intricate social relationships of their former environment. But women who remained within the family circle of the heathen home encountered many problems of adjustment. Already in the time of Paul the converted wife married to a non-Christian husband who objected to her new religion was tempted to cut the Gordian knot by means of divorce, a move explicitly discouraged by Paul. His view of the brief period during which she would have to endure her embarrassing situation until Christ would presently return to dissolve all worldly relations, led him to advise the Christian men or women not to seek immediate release from an unbelieving companion. By all possible means

---

[27] Plutarch would have a married woman revere only those gods approved by her husband (*Conjugal Precepts,* xix).

121

the marriage bond should be maintained, with the hope of bringing one's heathen wife or husband into Christianity. This was the rule laid down by Paul for all his converts.[28]

The church in later years adherred to the Pauline ideal. In instances of extreme difficulty the Christian partner, especially the wife, sometimes resorted to divorce, as did the Roman lady whose rejected husband vented his wrath on Christianity by bringing about the arrest and execution of Ptolemæus and Lucius.[29] But the character of this man was such that in all probability his wife would have divorced him even if she had not attached herself to a new religion. In general, however, the married woman on becoming a Christian did not seek to break the usual ties of home. Her position must often have been one of great difficulty, sometimes involving her in compromise with heathen customs frowned upon by the more rigorous Christian teachers; but, thanks to her tact and fidelity, she has to be given a large measure of credit for making Christianity welcome and respectable in the home-life of the ancient world.

To strike the proper balance of loyalty between one's family connections and one's duty to the church was always a delicate problem. The question had become acute before the close of the first Christian century. Christian teachers soon recognized that their religion was likely to be a disruptive influence in the family,

[28] I Cor. 7:10-17.
[29] Justin, *Apology* II. 2.

and they encouraged converts to make loyalty to Christianity the primary consideration. They cited the example of Jesus in breaking his own family ties and they reported words of his confirming their experience that one's bitterest foes might be the members of one's own household.[30] The situation was particularly trying in times of persecution. While a father or mother, a son or a daughter, might have been ready to suffer imprisonment or execution had personal feeling alone been involved, the consequences for loved ones must often have deterred a convert from pursuing his new religious loyalty to its fatal conclusion.[31] But the ideal procedure always called for the sacrifice of family rather than of faith. Love of children must not be placed above love for the Lord; one must renounce parents, relatives and all things in this world in order to attain unto true life.[32]

Fortunately, in the course of social growth adjustments and compromises were so successfully effected

[30] Mark 3:31-35; Matt. 10:34-42; Luke 12:51-53.

[31] Note, for example, the heartrending story of Felicitas, resisting the pleas of her aged father on behalf of himself and her infant son, told so vividly in the *Passion of Perpetua and Felicitas,* and now easily accessible in the rendering of E. C. E. Owen, *Some Authentic Acts of the Early Martyrs* (Oxford, 1927), pages 78 ff. She was about twenty-two years old, of noble family and liberal education and married to a husband of her own rank; her father and mother and two brothers were still living, and she had an infant son at her bosom, yet she stoutly refused to recant and chose rather the glory of a martyr's death in 203 A.D. Not every Christian thus situated would have been so persistent in refusing the easy means of escape, a tendency that the publication of *Acts of the Martyrs* was clearly designed to offset. On this point see especially D. W. Riddle, *The Martyrs: A Study in Social Control* (Chicago, 1931).

[32] Eusebius, *History,* VI. 41. 18; *Didascalia,* XIX.

that Christianity was able to endure without requiring the abolition of the family as an institution existing in the Roman world. The wives and daughters in many a heathen home adopted the Christian religion during the second and third centuries without separating themselves from the family. Among these, indeed, there was a surprisingly large number of representatives from the higher classes. Ladies of the nobility, whose privilege it was to be called *"clarissimæ,"* wives of high government officials, and women of wealth and social position were to be found in considerable numbers in the Christian congregations in the larger cities in the third century. Their husbands were not always pleased with this situation, yet as a rule they seemed to have been either tolerant or indifferent. It was characteristic of imperial society in this period for women to exercise great freedom in their choice of religious cults, and their patronage had contributed in no small measure to the popularity of other Oriental religions even before Christianity appeared on the scene. Heathen men were not accustomed to trouble themselves greatly about the religious affiliations of their women-folk, so long as the life of the home was not disrupted. Even many priests of the pagan cults in the fourth century are said to have had Christian wives, whose children and servants were attached to the church.[33]

Some Christian preachers viewed with alarm the conduct of those ladies who were engaged in solving

[33] Sozomen, V. 16, reports that the Emperor Julian lamented this fact.

124

the practical difficulty of maintaining social respectability along with their espousal of Christianity. They dressed in style and maintained pleasant contacts with non-Christian acquaintances in a way that shocked the rigorous Tertullian and Cyprian, or even the more tolerant Clement of Alexandria. Tertullian, who was almost vicious in his judgments of the "weaker sex," bitterly condemned all female adornments. Could he have had his way, undoubtedly he would have denied to Christian women any social intercourse with persons outside of the church. He ordered his own wife to dress so plainly and deport herself so sedately that no other man could possibly find her attractive. But evidently he had an observing eye for feminine adornments, even if only to furnish a target for his sarcasm. He charged that the well-to-do Christian ladies of Carthage dressed as smartly as did their heathen friends, wearing bracelets, anklets, and pearl or emerald necklaces. Apparently some self-assertive ladies whom he had criticized made bold to defend themselves on the ground that it was socially advantageous for Christianity to have its representatives dress in fashion. He was incapable of appreciating the point. Rather, he would have had Christian women prepare their wrists for prison shackles, their ankles for the stocks, and their necks for the sword in the time of persecution.

In their conformity to social custom the Christian ladies were, perhaps, even wiser than they knew. At any rate, they made their distinctive contribution toward struggling Christianity's growing social prestige, without sacrificing so completely as critics of Tertullian's temper very sincerely feared, the moral and spiritual values of their religion. But the difficulties were further enhanced by the presence in the church of unmarried persons, especially young women, belonging to the higher social ranks. In the closing decades of the second century there was already a manifest tendency among Christian girls to marry heathen young men, a practice against which Tertullian, as we should expect, felt it necessary to utter a vigorous protest. He had no sympathy with the attitude of his more liberal contemporaries who tolerated this procedure. Yet the custom continued and half a century later called forth the disapproval of Cyprian, who declared that marriage with pagans must not be consummated.[34] But the problem resisted solution. At the close of the third century the synod of Elvira reiterated the admonition against mixed marriages; although marriageable maidens in the church had become numerous, they were not to be joined in wedlock to heathen husbands.[35]

Had these regulations been strictly observed it would have meant the loss of caste in Roman society for many young women now attached to Christianity. The traditional attitude of the Roman world was uncompromising in this matter. If a maiden in a senatorial family married beneath her station she lost her right to the title *"clarissima."* It was as if the daughter of

[34] Cyprian, *Testimonies,* III. 62.
[35] *Canon* 15.

126

some socially distinguished family today should marry so humbly in the social scale that the public would no longer refer to her as "Miss" but would dub her simply "Bridget" or "Hilda." And the difficulty was further augmented by the fact that a marriageable young man of her own class was hardly to be found in the church. There were many men of high character and good habits in the Christian society, but among them the number was relatively few who equaled in social status the young women attached to the church.

Heathen society had surmounted this artificial barrier of custom by means of the institution of concubinage. Two young people of different rank, who might not legally marry, entered the state of concubinage with full social approval. The relation between the contracting parties might be as true and devoted as that of legal wedlock. Some Christians followed this custom, although it was never generally approved by the leaders of the church. Where these negative counsels prevailed the Christian girls of high rank were faced by the probability that the large majority of them would have to forego wedlock, and thus ultimately would be cut off from family life and participation in the activities of gentile society at large. Apparently many of them refused to accept this fate and chose rather to be joined in marriage to desirable heathen husbands.

The practice of concubinage seems to have been less popular, notwithstanding the stamp of virtual approval placed upon it by that liberally disposed bishop of

Rome, Callistus, early in the third century. He advised Christian maidens, who wished to retain legal right to their social rank, that, preferably to marrying a heathen of their own social status, they should unite themselves in the state of concubinage with a worthy Christian slave or free man of lower rank, and the bishop would pronounce the ecclesiastical blessing upon the union. For this attitude he was severely criticized by his purist opponent, Hippolytus.[36] Whether the action of Callistus is to be interpreted as a deliberate defiance of the marriage laws of the Roman state, or as a mere concession to practical circumstances within the Christian society, his precedent was not generally followed and was definitely condemned in later times.[37] The dilemma generally faced was a choice between perpetual maidenhood and marriage with a heathen man. The former alternative was zealously advocated by many Christian preachers, while the latter was preferred by many Christian maidens.

Mixed marriages were by no means a social liability for Christianity. On the contrary, they opened up a channel for its further expansion in the Roman world even though the evangelistic zeal of these Christian women in their new heathen environment cannot always be described as "apostolic." But it was not without important consequences for the social advancement of the new religion. The husband respected, or was

[36] *Refutation* IX. 12. 24.
[37] See *Apostolic Constitution*, VIII. 32. 13; 34. 13; Leo I, *Epistle* 167, Quest. 4.

indifferent toward, the religion of his wife, who was free to bring up the children in her own faith. Her situation must often have presented difficulties, and have called for compromises, but it was hardly so hopeless as might be assumed from the exaggerated form in which it was over-zealously described by the fiery and sarcastic Tertullian.[38] Not only in the home, but in the wider social contacts of the community, this Christian wife and mother was in a peculiarly strategic position to demonstrate the livable and praiseworthy character of the new religion. Her activity did not appeal to writers of martyrologies, but often her life was none the less heroic and her service to the social establishment of the Christian cause may have been far greater than has ever yet been imagined.

In the wider contacts of the community Christians were confronted by many nice questions of procedure. Could a Christian family maintain social intercourse with other families who had not accepted the new religion? Life in the Roman world among persons of the same rank and occupation in a community was characterized by much sociability displayed in the hospitality of the home, in the mingling of friends at the spectacles, and in the fellowship of the festivities at the temples on numerous holidays throughout the year. People who had stood high in the social esteem of their neighbors could not readily consent to sacrifice their position in the community when they entered the church, and by the close of the second century even

[38] See particularly his *To His Wife* II. 1-7.

129

the more rigorous disciplinarians were forced to recognize the necessity of adjustments in their attitude on this practical issue. Christians must, of course, avoid soiling their souls by contact with idolatrous customs. But it would have been an exaggerated flaunting of their sense of superior righteousness to decline an invitation to a birthday celebration, or a marriage anniversary, or a wedding feast, at the home of life-long friends who had not taken up with Christianity and yet had no desire to ostracize their respected Christian neighbors. If a Christian guest were excused from participating in any idolatrous rites performed on the occasion, he need not absent himself from the social assemblies of his heathen friends. A member of the church who had scruples against partaking in the religious part of a family celebration could close his eyes to that phase of the performance, as a teetotaler in modern times at a festive gathering may turn down his glass when the wine is served. Otherwise a Christian could make himself an agreeable participant in the festivities. He did not need to be an insufferable bore, even though he did not aspire to be "the life of the party."

The conciliatory procedure in social relations had its dangers for the church, a fact quickly perceived by many preachers. They protested against the temptation to laxity in moral standards, and pointed to concrete instances in which disaster had followed. These warnings had to be frequently renewed as the practice of freer social intercourse with non-Christians became

130

more general. Members of the church yielded to the social urge within what they regarded as proper limits, which sometimes were rather elastic. Yet their conduct on the whole won them increasing respect in the community at large, and consequently strengthened the popularity of the religion they had espoused. On occasion they were to be found in the company of their neighbors at the public festivities on religious holidays, although they absented themselves from those parts of the celebration that constituted specific acts of heathen worship. Nor did they refrain from attending the spectacles, such as the popular chariot races. They felt no impropriety in sharing in the play-life of the community, while avoiding, of course, the baser theatrical performances and the bloody gladiatorial exhibitions. But athletic contests in the stadium, a thrilling performance in the circus, and other customary recreations, could, they felt, be legitimately enjoyed by Christians as well as by heathen. For a rigorist like Tertullian, who would have denied members of the church the emotional satisfaction of witnessing a chariot race, they had a ready reply; had not Elijah himself ridden in a chariot on his way to heaven?

IV

The Christian movement had early drawn into itself a few converts from the upper classes. Apparently there were some people of this type in the group at Corinth. Although they were conspicuously in the minority, and were treated with scant courtesy by Paul, he recognized

131

a sprinkling of cultured, influential, and well-born persons in the Corinthian congregation. Gaius, who entertained the Apostle and at whose house the congregation assembled, and Stephanas, may have been persons of social importance, while another Corinthian Christian, Erastus, occupied the office of city treasurer.[39] Perhaps these persons were among the leaders who had caused trouble by their admiration for the more polished oratory of Apollos in contrast with the less elegant discourses of Paul. And they, naturally, would have been most ready to appreciate the desirability of securing for their cause the paid services of a Christian orator—a "wise man" (sophist) as he was termed in those days—in preference to the occasional and gratuitous ministrations of a traveling evangelist "weak of bodily presence and contemptible of speech."[40] Whether the earliest missionaries had desired it or not, the new religion had attracted some cultured and socially prominent people.

During the last quarter of the first century several persons of good social standing were known to have been connected with Christianity. The writer of Acts informed Theophilus that "not a few women of the first rank" had responded favorably to Christian preaching in Thessalonica, while in Berea, among the many who believed, there were "not a few Greek women of good standing, and men." And at Athens,

[39] Rom. 16:23.
[40] II Cor. 10:10 and I Cor., Chaps. 1-4. According to Acts 18:24, Apollos was an "eloquent man who was mighty in the Scriptures."

although the philosophers in general rejected the Christian message, a convert had been secured from among the members of the Areopagus court.[41] Before the close of the century a few persons of rank at Rome, like Pomponia Græcina, whom Tacitus calls a "lady of distinction,"[42] and the consul Titus Flavius Clemens with his wife Domitilla,[43] had embraced Christianity. But the number of such persons was relatively few, in comparison with converts from the lower ranks.

During the second and following centuries Christianity attracted increasingly larger numbers from among the upper classes. They were still only a minority in comparison with the total membership of the Christian communities, but their initiative and ability as leaders gave them an importance for the new cause quite out of proportion to their numbers. When in the latter part of the third century, and the first decade of the fourth, the church and the state came into violent conflict, the struggle was no longer one in which a crude superstition of the populace was being suppressed for the sake of civic purity in religious practices. On the contrary, it was a battle between two rival sections of the higher classes. The decrees of the persecutors were directed especially against members of the aristocracy who had espoused Christianity. Valerian, for example, in the year 258, had specified punishment especially for "Senators, members of the nobility and

[41] Acts 17:4, 12, 34.
[42] *Annals,* XIII. 32; probably Christianity was the "foreign superstition" she had been guilty of embracing.
[43] Dio Cassius, lxvii. 14.

133

Roman knights," who were to be demoted from their dignity and deprived of their property if they refused to abandon Christianity.[44]

Christians were now to be found holding positions of responsibility in the government, even in the army.[45] They were members of local city councils, or even of the Senate at Rome, and were held in honor at the imperial palace. During the forty years of comparative peace enjoyed by the church prior to the outbreak of the great Diocletian persecution in 303 A.D., Christianity's social position greatly improved. In the early half of the third century certain prominent members of the church had been prone to court the favor of the rulers, and had so busied themselves with these activities that Cyprian could say "most bishops, despising their divine administration, became administrators for secular rulers."[46] By this conduct the church had, in Cyprian's opinion, invited the calamity that fell upon it in the Decian-Valerian persecution. But when the crisis had passed the same disposition to mix in imperial affairs showed itself with renewed vigor.

Apparently Christians, if otherwise qualified for positions of social dignity, now found their religion no serious impediment to the full exercise of their privileges. Prominent Christians sometimes held high offices in the state, or were otherwise active in public

[44] Cyprian, *Epistle* 80 (81). 1. See below, page 185.
[45] Statistical data on these subjects may be found in A. Harnack, *Mission and Expansion of Christianity*, Vol. II, pages 42-64; and in the appropriate sections of C. J. Cadoux, *The Early Church and the World*.
[46] Cyprian, *On the Lapsed*, 6.

134

affairs. It is said even of Valerian that in the early part of his reign, before he instituted hostile action against Christianity in 257 A.D., his court was "a veritable church of God."[47] And after his death in 260 Christians again enjoyed for more than forty years continued favor at the imperial court. It was not uncommon to find them occupying official positions under the government and discharging important duties of state. Senators, knights, and persons of the aristocratic class in general suffered no inconvenience from their membership in the church, although as yet it does not appear that their attachment to Christianity constituted any social advantage. In the case of Paul of Samosata, bishop of Antioch, who held the office of *procurator ducenarius* while the city was subject to Zenobia of Palmyra, his deposition by Aurelian in 272 A.D. was not due to his Christian connections. On the contrary, he lost standing because he was not sufficiently subservient to the bishop of Rome, whose will the emperor apparently was glad to enforce.[48]

When Diocletian became emperor in 284 A.D. and began his extensive governmental reforms, the social respectability of Christianity was freely recognized in official circles. The emperor's wife and daughter were devoted to this religion, and it had numerous representatives in the court at his new capital, Nicomedia, in Bithynia.[49] The rhetorician Lactantius, and the

[47] Eusebius, *History*, VII. 10. 4.
[48] Eusebius, *History*, VII. 30. 19.
[49] Lactantius, *Death of the Persecutors*, 15.

135

grammarian Flavius, whom Diocletian called to Nicomedia from North Africa, as distinguished men of their respective professions, were Christians. By this time members of the church seem effectively to have overcome their earlier scruples regarding the holding of office under a heathen ruler. The reserve of men like Tertullian and Cyprian had been successfully outlived. Christians served as magistrates, finance ministers, mayors of cities, governors of provinces, or even held the office of *flamen* (the lighter of the sacrificial fires), apparently without forfeiting their right to membership in the church.

Specific examples of Christians who served in these capacities are not numerous, but are all the more significant on that account. One hears of a descendant of the Italian nobility who had become a Christian, yet held successive positions of dignity under the emperors and discharged in praiseworthy fashion the duties of magistrate and of finance minister. Another Christian of high social rank represented the imperial authority at Alexandria, where he daily administered justice accompanied by soldiers and all the characteristic displays of Roman officialdom. Whether Christians who served in these capacities previous to the recognition of Christianity by Constantine stood as high in the esteem of the church as they did after Christianity became the favored religion in the state may be questioned. At the earlier date they must have submitted to the observance of certain heathen religious formalities connected with the discharge of

136

their political duties, although they may have performed these rites in very perfunctory fashion. But it meant much for the advancement of Christianity's social prestige that these men, whose attachment to the new religion could hardly have been unknown by the authorities, were accepted and tolerated in office.[50]

Once Christianity was openly tolerated or zealously supported by emperors, the problem of its social standing in official circles was immediately solved. Henceforth its respectability in connection with the affairs of state was unquestioned. But there were wide cultural areas in Roman society that still remained to be won. Christianity could not rise to the fullest measure of dignity in ancient civilization until it had captured the aristocracy of philosophy, education, literature, and art.

The philosophers were a distinctly recognized class in imperial Roman society, but their prestige in the third and fourth centuries was not so great as it had been in earlier times. On the other hand, in the early centuries of the Christian era they were more widely

[50] Eusebius, *History*, VIII. 1-11 counts it an honor for Christians to have received this measure of recognition by pre-Constantinian emperors, and he remarks, evidently in an effort to justify the conduct of these Christians, that they had been excused from offering the sacrifices customary in connection with the discharge of their duties. One has a suspicion that Eusebius may have been idealizing at this point. Undoubtedly Christians had held office, but they may have done so by compromising on these external formalities. This procedure seems to be suggested by the action of the Council of Elvira (*canon* 56) which prohibits a Christian magistrate during the year of his duumvirate from participating in the rites of the church. Similarly, one may accept the office of *flamen*, but with certain restrictions on his Christian privileges.

dispersed than ever before over the lands around the Mediterranean, and their message had been extensively popularized for the benefit of the man on the street. This line of development had resulted in an increase of popular influence, which far outweighed any loss of prestige from abandoning the seclusion of the cloister. Christianity in the second century had been adopted by several persons who had previously been students of popular philosophy and who set themselves up as Christian teachers following the model of the contemporary philosophical lecturer. Naturally they undertook the public defense of Christianity against the calumnies and criticisms of its enemies.

While the support of the converted philosopher was a valuable aid to Christianity, his presence in the church did not bring it so large a measure of social prestige as one might at first sight imagine. In the eyes of heathen men of culture a Christian philosopher was a deserter of true wisdom, a renegade philosopher, since he had abandoned Homer and the Greek thinkers as fountains of wisdom and had given his first allegiance to the crude barbarian Moses. This the Christian teacher conceded, adding, however, that the wisdom contained in the Scriptures was far superior to anything possessed by the ancient Greeks. He alleged that Christianity, as a religion of revelation, was more worthy of respect than was the inferior wisdom of the greatest heathen scholars. Excepting a few items and persons, he pronounced wholesale condemnation upon the Greek philosophical inheritance, and explained that

138

its acceptable elements had ultimately a Hebrew origin. At best heathen learning was only a kind of dessert, of which Christians might partake after feasting on biblical wisdom.[51] A less sympathetic appraisal declared the wisdom of the Greeks to be empty and nonsensical—a fitting object of derision for the Christian wise man.[52]

These Christian scholars were much more appreciative of Greek wisdom and more largely indebted to it, than an outsider offended by their polemics could imagine. The effort to make Christianity popular by means of dialectics largely failed in the ancient world, as it has failed on many a mission field in later times. Not until the representatives of Christianity became more completely imbued with the cultural heritage of paganism, perhaps all unconsciously drawing inspiration therefrom, could they win the respect of their intellectual heathen contemporaries. Christians had to learn that an acceptable educational program for the Roman Empire could not confine itself to the Scriptures and ignore the Greek and Roman classics. Nor could Christian writers and speakers win a hearing among the cultured if they failed to acquire the literary skill of the Greek rhetorician or the Roman orator. Likewise the æsthetic poverty of early Christian worship had to make way for an artistic development in ritual, robes and buildings, before the new religion

[51] Clement of Alexandria, *Stromateis*, VI. 18.
[52] *E.g.*, Hermias, *Mockery of Heathen Philosophers.*

139

could satisfy the needs of people whose æsthetic tastes had been accustomed to find satisfaction in magnificent displays of pageantry exhibited in the religious rites connected with temples whose architectural beauty was the pride of many a community.

During the third and fourth centuries Christianity made rapid progress in the acquisition of these cultural values, and its social prestige mounted accordingly. The prejudice against the study of Greek and Roman literature, replete as it was with idolatrous imagery, was overcome. Christian teachers of the classics were to be found in the public schools in the fourth century, and a good literary education as a preparation for teaching or preaching Christianity became more and more highly prized.[53] When pressed for scriptural authority to justify this plundering of profane literature for the enrichment of Christianity, one had only to remember that God had instructed the Hebrews in their flight from Egypt to carry away for a more worthy use the gold and silver vessels of their enemies.[54] And it was also to be remarked that language was only the vehicle employed by Christianity to carry a new and infinitely more serious moral and spiritual message. Christians alleged that the heathen literary artist had been chiefly interested in form, while

[53] On the value of rhetoric to Christianity, see especially Lactantius, *Institutes*, V. 1. A century later Chrysostom in the East, and Ambrose and Augustine in the West, were masters in literary art. Even Jerome, in spite of his famous dream in which he was charged with being a Ciceronian rather than a Christian, could not shake off his pagan cultural heritage.

[54] Augustine, *Christian Doctrine*, II. 40.

140

they were primarily concerned with content. Yet when Ambrose, bishop of Milan in the latter part of the fourth century, composed a formal treatise on Christian morality to supplant heathen teaching on the subject, he appropriated not only the title, but also the general outline, as well as much of the content, of Cicero's famous work *De officiis*. It was fortunate for Christianity's social position among cultured people that Ambrose's procedure was now in good standing within the church.

The Christian religion was relatively late in the acquisition of artistic and architectural significance for ancient society. Buildings specially constructed and set apart for the services of the new religion first began to appear at the close of the second century. In the meantime the congregations met in private homes, or in the open air, or in like temporary quarters.[55] Small and unadorned buildings had to suffice in the early third century, nor did Christians as yet feel any inclination to ape the pagan temples which they despised.[56] But the second half of the third century witnessed a great increase in church building.[57] There was a pretentious structure housing Christian activities in the city of Nicomedia in the time of Diocletian. His destruction of Christian churches only cleared the ground for more elaborate buildings. Toleration under Constantine marked a new era in the history of Chris-

---

[55] *Acts of Justin*, III.
[56] Clement of Alexandria, *Stromata*, VII. 5.
[57] Eusebius, *History*, VIII. 1. 5.

tian architecture.[58] Stately buildings were reared and splendidly decorated within and without. The bishops encouraged the adornment of the "temple of God with suitable splendor, in order that the court of the Lord may be glorified."[59] The æsthetic character of the services was likewise improved. The enrichment of the ritual, the improvement of the music, the use of more elaborate ecclesiastical vestments, and similar concessions to the artistic tastes of antiquity found a home in the Christian church where they exerted a powerful influence in establishing its social respectability among the aristocratic and cultured people of the Roman Empire. The day was presently to arrive when social prestige was unattainable beyond the pale of the church.

[58] *Ibid.*, X. 3 f.
[59] Ambrose, *Duties of Clergy*, II. 21 (111).

142

IV. *Christianity and Politics*

IV

Christianity and Politics

THE TWO MOST FORMIDABLE INSTITUTIONS PRODUCED BY Roman society were the imperial system of political administration and the ancient Catholic church. Both establishments were popularly supposed to owe their origin and continued existence to the favor of heaven. State and church were alike sacred institutions; patriotism and piety were essentially religious attitudes. Loyalty to the state required full allegiance to its deities, and fidelity to the church necessitated whole-hearted reverence for its divine protectors.

Had Christians remained socially insignificant, their refusal to worship the Roman deities might easily have passed unnoticed. But when their distinctive manner of life aroused the hostility of their neighbors and made evident their unwillingness to support the customary religious activities of the community, future conflicts with the political guardians of society's welfare were rendered inescapable. In a world where both state and church were believed by their respective sponsors to be divine establishments, the conflict could not remain simply a struggle to preserve the integrity of one or another set of human values. Inevitably it became a battle of the gods to be fought out in a society whose welfare was thought to depend immediately and ultimately upon recognizing the dignity, and thus securing the goodwill, of the tutelary divinities.[1]

In the course of its rise to a position of social dignity within the Roman state, Christianity suffered from frequent outbursts of hostility on the part of the authorities. Its political status hung in the balances until it was officially tolerated early in the fourth century. Henceforth it enjoyed an increasing measure of patronage, and before the century closed it boldly claimed a position of dictatorship over the total religious and political activities of the Empire. The process of growth in this phase of the new religion's social triumph has now to be traced.[2]

I

The earliest Christians were quite unconcerned with politics. They had no ambition either to reform the Roman government or to capture positions of influence in the administration. For a long time they were doubtful regarding the propriety of receiving into full church membership persons so closely associated with heathen-

[1] This subject has been discussed more fully in S. J. Case, *Experience with the Supernatural in Early Christian Times* (New York, 1929), pages 186-220: "Protection for Society."

[2] Literature on the relations between Christianity and the Roman state is abundant. The subject is treated in the appropriate sections of several books cited above on page 47, note 4, especially Benigni, Bigelmair, Cadoux, Troeltsch. Representative works on the persecutions of Christianity by the Roman authorities are listed in S. J. Case (editor), *A Bibliographical Guide to the History of Christianity* (Chicago, 1931), items 466-474. See also A. Causse, *Essai sur le conflit du christianisme primitif et de la civilisation* (Paris, 1920); L. Homo, *Les empereurs romains et le christianisme* (Paris, 1931).

ism as was necessarily the case with those who remained in the employ of the state. It was not easy for an official to follow in daily life the pattern of conduct set up by Christianity. But if he were willing to undertake this task he was welcomed into the church. And if he exerted his political influence on behalf of his fellow-believers, that service was gratefully appraised. Early Christian concern with political issues did not extend beyond these personal activities. No one as yet seems ever to have regarded the conversion of a government official as the entering wedge opening up the way for Christianity to exert its corporate influence upon the administration.

Until local representatives of the government in different parts of the empire showed themselves ready from time to time to use force against the Christians, the attitude of the latter toward the state was one of respectful toleration. Although the Roman administration was not thought by Christians to be an essential and permanent good, something necessary to the well-being of society for all time to come, yet it belonged to the present natural order which the Christian God momentarily used to serve his own inscrutable purposes. Even though Satanic forces in politics were at present enjoying a self-assumed autonomy, which would grow bolder and more assertive as the fatal hour for their final overthrow drew nearer, God had not surrendered supreme control; and all the benefits experienced by Christian missionaries in the relatively well-governed Roman state were therefore accepted as blessings ultimately derived from the Deity whom the Christians revered.

This political philosophy of Christians enabled them in all good conscience to believe that they were the most loyal and useful citizens to be found in the emperor's domains. This did not mean that he and his representatives in the government were essentially Christian, or would ever as a class become members of the church. In their official capacity as rulers of this world they were primarily servants of Satan and destined to fall more and more under his demonic sway; "all the kingdoms of the world and the glory of them" belonged to the devil who could give them to whomsoever he would.[3] But the activity of Christians in the world was convincing evidence that God had not completely abandoned the work of his creation. In fact, the rise of Christianity was concrete proof of the divine plan to bring the old order to a close with the establishment of a new regime of perfect bliss. In so far as God was temporarily employing the Roman state toward this end, by inspiring those orderly procedures in society that made possible the success of the Christian enterprise, he was really bestowing his favor upon the political rulers. Had they not been deceived by Satan they might have turned at once to Christianity. But for at least two centuries the obstacles to Christian success in the Roman Empire were so gigantic that no Christian could visualize the possibility of a

[3] Matt. 4:8 f.; Luke 4:5 f.

148

Roman emperor's conversion. Then, too, any such event would have upset the whole scheme of apocalyptic thinking that seemed essential to Christian theology while the new religion remained a socially unpopular and severely persecuted movement.[4]

In the meantime Christians, being friends of the true God, were friendly toward all agencies operating to maintain order in the Roman state. The Christian ideal, tersely set forth in a familiar passage in Paul's letter to the Roman church, unreservedly demanded respectful obedience to the authorities.[5] This attitude was consistently maintained until a measure of revision was necessitated by the circumstances of persecution. Even then the general principle was not altered. Obedience to political authorities was always a recognized Christian obligation, to be carefully discharged in all matters not affecting one's religious loyalties. The ordinary laws of the state were to be obeyed; the faithful payment of all taxes and tribute was enjoined; Christians were urged to be on their guard against any secular acts that might bring them in disfavor with the

[4] For example, Tertullian, at the close of the second century, thought Cæsars would have believed on Christ "if Cæsars had not been necessary to this age, or if it had been possible for Cæsars to be Christians" (*Apology,* xxi). But this could never come to pass. All regal splendor had been rejected by Christ; "what he rejected he damned, what he damned he reckoned as devilish ostentation" (*Idolatry,* xviii). Tertullian was looking forward to the day when he would be privileged to behold all Cæsars writhing in the fires of hell (*Spectacles,* xxi).

[5] Rom. 13:1-7. For the opinion that there were Christians in Rome who, under the influence of Jewish heritages, took an openly hostile attitude toward all worldly governments, see H. Weinel, *Die Stellung des Urchristentums zum Staat* (Tübingen, 1908), pages 14 f.

149

authorities. In a word, daily conduct in all normal relations with the government was to be beyond reproach, even beyond suspicion.

The presence of the Jews in Roman society, and the popular feeling among the officials that Jewish residents in a gentile community were a constant menace to the public peace, furnished an additional incentive for Christians to stress their law-abiding disposition. The original gentile opinion that Christianity was simply a new Jewish sect, and local disturbances caused by the rivalry between synagogue and church, made the position of the Christians especially difficult. They needed to prove by all possible means that they were not a menace to the good order of the state. This critical situation was fully appreciated by their leaders in the early years of the movement's career on gentile soil. Evidently the writer of the Book of Acts had this problem in mind when he took pains to bring to the attention of Theophilus illustrations of early contacts between Roman officials and Christian missionaries in which the former had found the new religion to be harmless and had shown toward it a distinctly friendly attitude. Probably the same motive inspired a disposition in certain Christian circles to relieve Pilate of a measure of responsibility for the execution of Jesus.

By every possible means Christians sought to show that they were peace-loving and obedient members of society. Nor were they content with this alone. They wished also to have it known that they had access to the supreme source of divine assistance, which they

150

gladly and gratuitously placed at the service of the government. In this they were entirely consistent with their convictions. If God was concerned to use the present governmental machinery as a means of preserving a temporary social order in which Christians might carry on a successful propaganda, it seemed quite proper that they on their part should make these human agencies an object of prayerful solicitation for the divine favor. Hence they not only obeyed rulers, but prayed to God on their behalf. They made intercession for all men, not forgetting to mention kings and all those who were in authority or intrusted with any administrative responsibilities, even though officials misused their authority and fell into the error of persecuting Christians. The persecutor, after all, was a Satanically deluded mortal who stood sadly in need of Christian prayers.

The example and precepts of Jesus were cited to justify prayer for the deceived persecutors.[6] Rulers and all officials were also remembered in the petitions of Christians.[7] In the time of Tertullian the entire well-being of the state seems to have been included in the scope of the church's prayers at Carthage. Christians besought their God to grant emperors long life, safety for their domains and households, valor in their soldiers, loyalty in the Senate, upright character in the citizens, a peaceful world, and everything that the

[6] Luke 23:34; cf. I Cor. 2:8; Acts 7:60; Matt. 5:11, 44; Luke 16:27.
[7] I Tim. 2:1-3; I Clement, 60. 2. 4; 61. 1 f.; Polycarp, *Phil.* 12. 3; Justin, *Apology*, I. 17. 3.

151

ruler as a man or a Cæsar could desire. Prayer was offered for his ministers and officials, for the prosperity of his times, for peace among his subjects, and for "delay of the end." By virtue of these petitions to the God of the Christians, they believed themselves to be the most valuable contributors to the safety of the state.[8]

The Christian attitude of passive respect for, and professed obedience to, the Roman government was constantly reaffirmed, even in periods of persecution. At the same time Christians made it apparent, by both word and deed, that in many respects the imperial government merited their disapproval, nor did they hesitate to prophesy its ultimate doom. While they credited its beneficial features to the overruling providence of their God, with equal confidence they ascribed its evils to Satan's activities in Roman society, and they boldly set themselves against him and all his works. His machinations were conspicuously displayed in the acts of violence against Christians. While this hostility endured, Christian preachers anathematized their persecutors, declared the antagonistic government to be a demonic invention, predicted a still greater decadence when Antichrist would temporarily hold sway throughout the Empire, and pictured its final destruction at the hands of the righteous God of the Christians.

[8] Tertullian, *Apology*, xxx. 4; xxxiii. 2; xxxix. 2. Cyprian, at his first trial, September 14, 257 A.D., informed the proconsul that Christians prayed to their God "for all men and for the safety of the emperors" (*Acts* I. 2).

Early Christianity had inherited from Judaism an extremely pessimistic type of opinion regarding the character of the contemporary political administration. But the perpetuation of this attitude within Christianity was no mere doctrinaire survival; frequently it seemed amply justified by the immediate experiences of Christians themselves living in the Roman Empire during the first three centuries. Under the imperial regime vice flourished, injustice was rampant, hosts of peoples served mammon rather than God, plunder and bloodshed knew no bounds even within the emperor's palace, the corrupting folly of idol worship pervaded society, while sacrilegious audacity reached its zenith in fierce persecution of the church of God. It involved no great stretch of the imagination, and was no resort to extravagant rhetoric, when a Christian declared the present to be "an evil age" saturated with wickedness, a "crooked generation" irredeemably corrupt, a world that lay "completely in the power of the Evil One."[9]

If the officials of the state, for whose reading the Christian apologists of the second century ostensibly composed their treatises in defense of Christianity, took the trouble to consult these books, they learned some very uncomplimentary things about themselves and their administration. In justice to the apologists it must be remembered that they were living in a day when the arrest and execution of Christians by the local au-

[9] *E.g.,* Gal. 1:4; Acts 2:40; I John 5:19. The New Testament books abound in similar statements. The Book of Revelation is the most vigorous in its condemnatory pronouncements, especially Chapters 16-20.

153

thorities was likely to occur at any moment, while emperors either approved or encouraged these acts of violence. Stung by the injustice of this procedure, the defenders of Christianity, although using courteous or even complimentary phrases in addressing emperors, did not hesitate to censure the rulers in language that was sometimes both defiant and threatening. By resisting almighty God the princes were bringing down upon their own heads, and upon the government they represented, the irresistible divine wrath. Misconduct demonstrated their senselessness, bigotry, and inhumanity.[10]

In their censure of heathen rulers the literary defenders of Christianity in the third century were still bolder and more drastic. The rapidity of Christianity's social growth inspired an increased confidence and vigor in its apologists, while lengthy periods of peaceful expansion gave it a new sense of power. The rulers along with their evil performances were declared to be destined for Hades. Temporarily they might seem to flourish, but presently they with all their glory would be cut down and wither away. In days of old God had determined the fate of the nations now unified under the central authority of Rome; the fierce anger of his indignation was about to be displayed in fulfillment of his prophecy that he would devour all the earth with the fire of his jealousy. Those who put

---

[10] *E.g.*, Aristides, 17; Justin, *Apology* I. 57. 3. As Tatian expressed it, "the constitution of the world is good, but its political administration is abominable" (*Against the Greeks* xix. 2).

154

their trust in the dignity, power, and wealth of rulership were hanging on the brink of magnificent disillusionment.[11]

The immoralities of imperial rule were portrayed in vivid colors. Injustice, extravagance, luxury, and licentiousness were declared to be outstanding features in the life of the governing classes. Human beings were slaughtered like mere animals; kings were more ready for carnage than were the most vicious wild beasts.[12] Virgil might say that "slaughter and swords were incessant" in the cruel age of antiquity, but Christians saw no cessation of these perversities even in Rome's golden age of imperial domination. Cæsars were more voluptuous than the notorious ancient kings, Physcon and Sardanapalus, had been.[13] Critics recalled with approval that the Book of Revelation had likened Rome to a harlot.[14] The administration in every city of the empire was dominated by "superstitious, licentious, and wicked men."[15] Taxation was exorbitant, avarice raged without restraint, judges were venal, no respect was paid to the rights of life or property. So Christian critics boldly alleged.

In earlier times Christians had found it desirable to stress their law-abiding disposition, but in the third and early fourth century they were more openly criti-

[11] Typical exponents of these sentiments are Clement of Alexandria, *Instructor*, II. 3.36; Hippolytus, *Daniel*, III. 4.1-4; Novatian, *Trinity*, 20; Origen, *Celsus*, VIII. 72; Cyprian, *Donatus*, 13.
[12] Hippolytus, *Daniel*, II. 4.2; III. 8.3-10; IV. 2.1-3.
[13] Tertullian, *Pallium*, iv.
[14] Tertullian, *Apparel of Women*, ii. 12; Hippolytus, *Antichrist*, 36.
[15] Origen, *Celsus*, III. 29.

cal of Roman legislation. They never conceded it to be of divine origin, yet their theologians commonly agreed with the Stoics in holding that all law was by nature the work of Deity.[16] But Christians affirmed more specifically that their God was the maker of all valid laws for men. When the decrees of the Roman government ran counter to the will of the divine legislator there was only one course of action open to Christians. They must disobey. Their disobedience might be only passive, but it was none the less unyielding. The bolder critics even in the second century had ventured severe criticisms upon the imperial legal system. It absurdly demanded of Christians a reverence for ancient laws that the Romans themselves now flagrantly transgressed.[17] In his *Address to the Greeks*[18] Tatian had categorically condemned all gentile legislation, pointing out its inconsistencies, injustices, and weaknesses. Christians transcended all the feeble enactments of men and regulated their living according to the perfect and incontrovertible laws of God. Thus they justified their refusal to accede to the demands of their persecutors, while maintaining the validity of their claim to be the most law-abiding people in the empire.

In the third century criticism became more aggressive as Christians more boldly asserted the right of recognition for their own legislative standards. Whether the laws of the Roman state were actually competent to

[16] See above, p. 28.
[17] Tertullian, *Apology*, vi. 1-9.
[18] xxviii.

156

suppress evil deeds was called in question,[19] and certainly in practice they had sadly failed. Even in that sanctum of Roman justice, the forum itself, one daily witnessed fraud, quarrels, venality, cruelty, and the miscarriage of justice generally.[20] Christians, who held themselves accountable to God only, could never be overawed by the dignity of earthly rulers.[21] When Origen in his comments on Romans came upon the passage in which the apostle had decreed explicitly that "he who resists authority resists the ordinance of God," Origen remarked that manifestly Paul had not intended Christians to obey the persecutors, for he had also said that "one ought to obey God rather than men." Moreover, Christians had now become so definite a unit in society that they were as justly entitled to live in accordance with their distinctive type of legislation within the Roman Empire as would have been the case if they had found themselves settled among a barbarian people like the Scythians. Disobedience was obligatory in the area of religion, and might be necessary even in other matters.[22]

Christians directed their bitterest criticisms against the religious sanctions of the government. Contemporary polytheism was condemned outright and stoutly resisted. There could be no deviation from the Pauline statement that while there were many gods and many lords revered among the gentiles, Christians could wor-

[19] Clement of Alexandria, *Stromateis*, VII. 3. 19.
[20] Cyprian, *Donatus* 10.
[21] Hippolytus, *Daniel*, I. 26. 2.
[22] Origen, *Celsus*, I. 1; V. 37.

ship only their own God revealed in the Old Testament and their own Lord Jesus Christ.[23] The adoration of idols was not only mere folly, but was the worship of the evil demons by whom all the rites of polytheism were inspired. The idol might be "nothing," but the demon it represented was a grave reality on whom Christianity declared a war to the death. When emperors, or other human dignitaries,[24] were made the object of worship, by ascribing to them deific epithets and by the adoration of their images, the procedure was thoroughly Satanic. Early Christianity on gentile soil remained too loyal to its theological heritage from Judaism, and too acutely conscious of the evils in its heathen environment, to be able to come to terms with the deities of the Roman state.

The immoralities of polytheism gave Christians the greatest of offense. Theologians might discuss in abstract terms the correct way of thinking about Deity, but the ordinary man in the church validated his convictions by more practical tests. For the great mass of Christians these tests were primarily moral and emotional rather than intellectual or rational, and were correspondingly more powerful in controlling the daily conduct of the average man. He believed, like everybody else in the Roman world except the Epicureans, that all the values in personal and social experiences had supra-mundane sanctions.[25] Hence the good and

[23] I Cor. 8:5 f.; cf. I Thess. 1:9 f.
[24] See above, pages 30 ff.
[25] See above, pages 27 ff.

estimable things in his experience as a Christian, and the evil and repulsive features in the heathen life about him, determined his convictions regarding the gods. He found life in the Christian society good, hence its deities—God and Christ, to whom some Christians added "good angels"[26]—were the proper objects of his reverence. Having found asylum in the church, he readily convinced himself that the hostile forces in his environment were instigated by evil powers utterly unworthy of his respect. When they brought about persecution of Christians they only demonstrated further their inherently demonic character.

Christian philosophers supplemented the common man's distrust of the gods of the Roman state with moral and rational criticisms of idolatry. Apologists never wearied of pointing out the absurdity of worshiping man-made idols. At other times they stressed the devilish character of the gods whom the idols represented, and upbraided the greed of these demons in demanding sacrifices. Traditional heathen beliefs about the deities were declared to be ridiculous and debasing. It was the height of folly to worship as heroic divinities men whether dead or living, and the gross immorality attributed to the great gods in the popular mythology rendered them more disgusting than adorable. The morality of the worshiper could not be expected to rise above that of his deities, hence the utterly debasing character of all polytheism. In the final analysis the total range of wickedness in the Roman world

[26] Justin, *Apology*, I. 6.

159

found its source in the state's subservience to the official gods.

It is quite possible, however, that the political authorities would have paid slight if any attention to their Christian literary critics, if the rank and file of the church membership had not put into actual practice the Christian principle of abstention from polytheism. Very soon this Christian procedure struck at the pride as well as the prosperity of every community where any considerable group of Christians assembled. And when it became known that they would refuse to acknowledge the lordship of Cæsar, their attitude implied an actual readiness to set themselves above the authority of the state. Until early in the fourth century their explanation of the propriety and the harmlessness of their conduct, from which even positive benefits were said to accrue to the government, proved unconvincing to emperors. In the meantime intermittent periods of sharp conflict between Christianity and the political authorities were to be expected.

II

The state was always the aggressor in its conflicts with the Christian church. Such, at least, was the outward fact. But the political authorities certainly believed that their hostility was amply justified by Christian provocations. The reasons for the government's suspicion and harsh treatment of Christianity are not easy, at least on first sight, to understand. In the Roman Empire a multitude of religions flourished unmolested, and it seems hardly conceivable that hostile action against Christians would ever have been initiated for reasons of mere religious prejudice.

In general the attitude of the imperial rulers toward various religions was tolerant and sometimes cordial. The official gods of the state were only partly native to Rome, or even to Italy; several of them had been imported from abroad. At the outset the Roman people were not at all adequately stocked with divine protection for the many new interests and activities that emerged in the course of political and commercial expansion issuing in world-empire. Since the primary function of Roman religion was not to render worship to specific deities, but was to insure divine protection for society, the growth of the pantheon had to keep pace with the progress and increasing complexity of national developments. The state was as ready to adopt new deities, who gave promise of being serviceable, as it was to annex new territories that seemed advantageous to national expansion.[27]

Foreign gods were officially naturalized at Rome, and became proper objects of worship for all citizens, by a formal action of the Senate. The cults of the new

[27] This essential characteristic of Roman religion has been recognized especially since the publication of T. Mommsen's article, "Der Religionsfrevel nach römischem Recht," *Historische Zeitschrift* LXIV (1890), pages 389-429. But the extent to which Oriental cults found themselves at home in the Empire was not adequately appreciated until F. Cumont's *Les religions orientales dans le paganisme romain* (Paris, 1906), English translation, *Oriental Religions in Roman Paganism* (Chicago, 1911), appeared. Further literature on the subject will be found in S. J. Case, *A Bibliographical Guide to the History of Christianity* (Chicago, 1931), items 425-441.

161

deities were placed under the control of the chief priest of the state, the *pontifex maximus*, the temple was built and maintained at public expense, and sacred days for the celebration of the rites were duly authorized. By this orderly procedure, not only all the principal gods of Greece, but Oriental divinities also, had been incorporated into the national religion even before the establishment of the Empire under Augustus. And still other cults, not officially recognized, had made their way into Rome itself as a result of the large foreign elements in its population. So long as these new religions did not trespass upon the city's sacred quarter, the *pomerium*, and did not draw away persons of Roman citizenship from loyalty to the deities of the state, the intruding cults were in no serious danger of attack by the government. Under the Empire they increased rapidly and appealed strongly to many native Romans. As the franchise was now more widely extended, not only in Italy, but in the provinces, large numbers of persons holding the dignity of citizenship were to be found worshiping at the shrines of foreign gods.[28]

The Romans had no jealous gods. It was not imagined that any deity in their official pantheon would feel offended when to his customary religious

[28] During the first two centuries of imperial rule foreign cults were private in character, but after Marcus Aurelius they increasingly received official recognition. Caracalla admitted not only Isis, but all foreign divinities, within the *pomerium*. Beginning with Aurelian, worship of the Syrian sun god (*sol invictus*) was chiefly favored, but was later pushed into the background by the popularity of Mithraism. See G. Wissowa, *Religion und Kultus der Römer* (second edition, München, 1912).

activities a citizen simply added worship at the temple of the Egyptian Isis or attendance upon the services in a Jewish synagogue. On the contrary, this display of supererogatory piety might well deserve praise. It meant, from the characteristically Roman point of view, that persons thus devout were drawing down into the service of the state new increments of divine assistance. These additional benefactors might be frail indeed, in comparison with the mighty deities formally recognized by the state, but no sort of supernatural help was too insignificant to be despised by a society whose troubles were so rapidly multiplying as were those of the Roman government, especially during the second and third centuries of the Christian era. A general persecution of all foreign cults would have been a wholly abnormal procedure on the part of the Roman state, and quite inconsistent with its fundamental religious policies.[29]

At the same time, attention to religious affairs was a primary duty of the political administration. Examples of disaster to the state in consequence of a neglect of religion on the part of persons in authority were

[29] Note the clear statement regarding the all-embracing religious policy of the Roman set forth by their spokesman in Minucius Felix, *Octavius,* VI f. By adopting the rites of all conquered peoples, and by strictly observing ancient religious customs, the Roman power had come to embrace the whole world, "extending beyond the rising and the setting of the sun and the limits of the ocean itself." The conqueror had recognized "the rites of all religions either out of gratitude for divine favors, or to avert the threatening wrath of the gods, or to appease their actual anger and fury." Owing to this comprehensive policy in religion, the Romans had been intrusted by the deities with eternal dominion over the whole earth.

often vividly portrayed in Roman literature.[30] Emperors like Augustus, Marcus Aurelius, the Severii, Decius, Diocletian, who took the duties of administration most seriously, gave diligent heed to the task of restoring or strengthening the religious health of the Empire. It could not hope to survive and prosper without the largest possible measure of divine favor, a goal to be attained by devotion to the gods of the state and to such other divine agencies as might sympathetically supplement their benefactions. When cults were discovered whose rites or customs seemed a menace to society's economic, moral, or orderly procedures, or refused worship to the national deities, persecution became a religious duty of the rulers.

From time to time in the course of Roman history situations arose calling for the suppression of detrimental foreign cults. The need for caution had been felt as early as the last quarter of the fifth century B.C.[31] The Bacchic associations were forbidden in 186 B.C. Hostile action against the rites of the Egyptian Isis occurred several times during the first century B.C. and the first century A.D., notwithstanding the religion's growing popularity during this period. The disclosure of an unfortunate immoral act, in which a worthy Roman lady had been victimized by a venal priest, led Tiberius to order the expulsion of the cult from Italy, the crucifixion of the priests, and the demolition of

---

[30] Data on this subject may be found in S. J. Case "Religion and War in the Græco-Roman World," *American Journal of Theology*, XIX (1915), 179-199.

[31] Livy, IV. 30.

164

the temples.[32] The Jews also were repeatedly expelled from Rome. Yet these various outbreaks of persecution were only sporadic and were occasioned by specific and local causes. They were not attempts to obliterate completely from imperial society any foreign religion. Nor did they more than temporarily hinder the spread of any of the cults thus persecuted.

In the case of the Jews the situation was somewhat unique. They were a well-differentiated racial unit. Although their territory had been annexed, they were still, by Roman custom, entitled to retain their ancestral faith. Rome never demanded that conquered peoples abandon the worship of their ancestral gods. Drastic action was taken only in the event that a subjugated people's religion appeared to be a political menace, as when Claudius suppressed the Druids, or Titus destroyed the temple at Jerusalem, or Hadrian forbade the Jews to enter Jerusalem and forced them to pay to the temple of Jupiter Capitolinus in Rome the yearly tax formerly paid to their own temple. All that could normally be expected of the Jews was that they make sacrifice for the foreign ruler, which they did while the temple in Jerusalem still stood, and offer prayers for him at the services for worship in the synagogue.[33] But it was another matter when Roman citizens adopted foreign rites requiring them to forsake

[32] Josephus, *Antiquities,* XVIII. 3. 4; Tacitus, *Annals,* II. 85.

[33] Josephus, *Apion* II. 77; *War* II. 197; Philo, *Gaius,* XXIII. 157; XXX. 231; XL. 317; XLV. 356; *Flaccus,* VII. 49. Cf. S. J. Case, *Jesus Through the Centuries* (Chicago, 1932), pages 59 ff.

165

their ancestral deities. This was the serious menace involved in Jewish proselytism. From the Roman standpoint, Judaism virtually meant religious denationalization of its gentile converts. But the Roman government did not demand religious denationalization of the Jews. So far as religion was concerned, they remained free to observe their ceremonies and were granted many concessions as a socially recognized unit in the Roman world.

When Christianity first came to the notice of the Roman officials it was assumed to be merely a Jewish sect. Had it restricted its efforts simply to the conversion of Jews, and produced no public disturbances threatening the peace of local communities, undoubtedly it would have continued to enjoy the same degree of immunity and toleration that the authorities had conceded to Judaism. But this possibility was soon eliminated. The rivalry between synagogue and church early became acute, and tended to assume riotous expression, thus incurring the suspicion of the Roman police. Moreover, when the authorities became more fully apprised of the real character of the Christian propaganda, they learned that it drew gentiles away from the service of their ancestral deities to worship of the Jewish God and his associate divinity, Christ. Paul himself had so described the aim of the Christian missionary.[34] In the sight of the Roman government this was the same vicious type of proselytism of which the Jews had been guilty, but was being

[34] I Thess. 1:9 f.

166

conducted by persons who had forfeited their privileges within the recognized Jewish communities.

When the police and the magistrates were made fully aware of the fact that the Jewish synagogue and the Christian congregation had utterly disowned each other, Christians were no longer to be dealt with as members of a privileged social group, but merely as recalcitrant individuals. They no longer enjoyed, as did the Jewish congregations, the right of assembly and toleration of their refusal to worship the gods of the state. Their situation was similar to that of conscientious objectors within one of our modern nations in war-time. If those who object to war are so fortunate as to be members of a religious group, like the Quakers, whose objection to bloodshed is recognized by the state authorities, they may with impunity refuse to enter the army. But if they cannot prove their title to membership in the recognized social group, they are treated as mere individuals guilty of treason, even though they may belong to a much larger religious body which has failed as a corporate entity to pronounce against war. When Christians in the Roman Empire lost their social status as Jews, they were treated as individual recusants. Social standing had to be recovered by a long and tedious process of living among their neighbors before political toleration could be realized.

The Roman politicians, however religious or irreligious one may adjudge them to have been, were not theologians in any modern sense of that term. With

167

perhaps a few exceptions, like the Stoic emperor, Marcus Aurelius, or the Neoplatonic Julian, they were not concerned to maintain the truth or falsity of any particular form of belief about deity. Their interests were strictly practical. The deities to be worshiped were those who insured the integrity and prosperity of the state. And since the state was an old institution, its divine protectors were the ancient gods. The institution had undergone many changes in the course of its evolution, as had the forms and functions of the gods, but the consciousness of specific changes was far less acute than the sense of social continuity. Hence the sacredness of tradition had to be defended, while novelties introduced in the course of political and religious evolution passed for revivals of ancient sanctions. And the ultimate test of the dogma's validity was the success of the state.

Christians, on the other hand, were thought harmful to the state. Their conduct was believed to be subversive of the best interests of the communities in which they dwelt. They refused to participate in its customary religious activities, they upset the economic balance by failing to purchase images or victims for sacrifice, they made no contributions to the treasures of the temples, they frowned upon the entertainments, they were clannish and unsocial, and who could say to what lengths their perversities might go when they assembled together in private? These observations would have been sufficient to convince the guardians of the political order that Christians were hateful to the state gods, even if Christian refusal to worship them had not become openly known. And when it was discovered, further, that they would not "offer incense before Cæsar's image,"[35] or swear by the "Fortune" or "Genius" of Lord Cæsar[36]—refusals signifying in the eyes of the Romans a disloyalty like that of the modern pacifist who in wartime fails to doff his hat to the flag—they concluded that these disobedient people should be incarcerated or executed. Punishment was necessary for the safety of the state, however insistently Christians might proclaim their innocence or their loyalty to emperors.

Before the year 250 A.D. hostile acts of the governmental authorities against the Christians were occasional in character and unauthorized by any specific imperial decree designed to apply to the whole of the empire. While approved or even instigated by the

[35] Pliny, *Letters,* X. 96.

[36] Apparently the demand to recognize "Lord Cæsar" first became embarrassing for Christians in the last decade of the first century under Domitian (Rev. 13:11-18). Insistence on an expression of loyalty to Cæsar was made doubly strong by further demanding that Christians "curse Christ," a requirement first explicitly attested by Pliny (about 112 A.D.). This was a very exceptional procedure for the Romans; no other religionists in the empire, not even Jews, were asked to renounce their own deities, even when required to pay any measure of respect to the gods of the state. But as yet Christians were so utterly lacking in any degree of social recognition that this special demand upon them as individuals is not surprising. On the rise and significance of emperor worship, see S. J. Case, *Evolution of Early Christianity* (Chicago, 1914), pages 195 ff.; also W. W. Fowler, *Roman Ideas of Deity* (New York, 1914), pages 81-133; E. Lohmeyer, *Christuskult und Kaiserkult* (Tübingen, 1919); "Kaiserkult," Pauly-Wissowa, *op. cit.,* Supplement Band IV (Stuttgart, 1924), cols. 806-853; Lily R. Taylor, *The Divinity of the Roman Emperor* (Middletown, Conn., 1931).

ruler, they were conditioned primarily by local circumstances and aimed at suppressing individual Christians in specific localities rather than at crushing Christianity as an institution throughout the whole of the empire.

The legal basis of the earlier procedures against Christians is uncertain. Three possibilities have been suggested.[37] Christians may have been haled into court as lawbreakers and found guilty of violating imperial legislation against such crimes as treason, sacrilege, membership in a foreign cult, or the practice of forbidden magic. Or a special law may have been promulgated, perhaps by Nero, in the form of an edict declaring Christianity to be an illicit religion.[38] Or the magistrates may have acted simply on their own responsibility, with the tacit or explicit approval of the emperor, in exercising the coercive power with which they were invested as guardians of the state's welfare in the localities over which they presided. The third of these possibilities seems to have been the more likely procedure on most occasions, yet it is certain that criminal charges of the first sort were made against

[37] The different theories have been conveniently summarized by A. Linsenmayer, *Die Bekämpfung des Christentums durch den römischen Staat bis zum Tode Kaisers Julian* (München, 1905), pages 27-43.

[38] This view rests on Tertullian's statements that Christianity's opponents cited as law *non licet esse vos* (Christianos), and that Nero had been the first emperor to take action against Christians (*Apology*, iv. 4; v. 3; *ad nationes*, i. 7). Also Trajan had approved of the action of Pliny, governor of Bithynia, in proceeding against Christians as such; but it must be noted that Trajan had also said Christians were "not to be sought out" and anonymous accusations were to be ignored (Pliny, *Letters*, X. 97).

170

Christians by the hostile populace. Nor could they prove themselves innocent when accused of holding unauthorized assemblies, or of unwillingness to worship either the ancient state gods or the emperor. And at a comparatively early date, when their attitude had become a matter of common knowledge, the magistrate needed only to make sure that a suspect stubbornly persisted in calling himself a Christian. Then the simple profession of "the name" might be punished without further ado. On the basis of the well-known attitude involved in this profession the court felt justified in taking action against these recalcitrant individuals long before any imperial decree had ever been issued prohibiting the Christian religion itself. As yet Christians, rather than Christianity, were being persecuted.

Popular animosity against Christians in specific localities preceded, and probably in most instances called forth, action by the authorities. Neither local government officials nor emperors were primarily responsible for initiating hostilities. The motivation was social rather than political, at least in the earlier stages of the conflict. The intervention of the state in the case of Jesus and of Paul had been largely brought about by the animosities of their compatriots; and Nero would hardly have thought it worth while to interfere with Christians in Rome had he not been able to capitalize their social unpopularity.[39]

Throughout the course of the early persecutions pop-

[39] See above, pages 102 ff.

171

ular hatred of Christians was constantly in evidence. The howling mob gloated over the misfortune of the arrested persons and hurled at them promiscuous accusations. One of the most damaging charges was "atheism," an indictment which Christians found it very difficult to refute. An apologist, writing in the quiet of his chamber, might succeed in composing a powerful philosophical refutation, pointing out that while Christians were atheists with respect to belief in the false gods of Roman religion, they were the most devout theists, in that they worshiped only the true God and his duly appointed agents.[40] But arguments of this sort had no weight with the mad populace, incensed by Christian refusal to support the traditional religious activities on which the heathen members of the community had always been accustomed to rely for happiness and prosperity.

Popular calumny knew no restraints; Christians were charged with every crime, social, moral, and religious, in the calendar of iniquities. They were said to be personally of no account—countrified, ignorant, boorish, wretched, unschooled, uncultured, unskilled, unfeeling, obtuse, stolid, fatuous, and obstinate people. Their aloofness from heathen society marked them as haters of mankind who audaciously set themselves up as a "third race" of men beside Jews and Gentiles. The Jews were "atheists," while Christians were super-atheists in their disdain for the divine protectors of Roman society. They were vicious impostors guilty of

[40] Justin, *Apology*, I. 6.

172

practicing magic and menacing with their spells everyone with whom they came in contact. They were themselves people possessed by an evil genius and purveyors of a foreign superstition, utterly evil, disorderly, detestable and mischievous. They were guilty of every vice —these stealthy people who loved darkness. In their secret mixed assemblies they practiced promiscuity, killed human infants and ate their flesh and drank their blood. They taught children to disobey their parents and to dishonor the customs of the ancients. They were a fatal disease, a living death, within the body politic, and their enemies vociferously urged the authorities to purge society of this evil. Christians were fit only for death by violence, suitable tinder for the fires of persecution, objects that invited slaughter with the sword, and appropriate bait for the wild beasts in the amphitheater. So their enemies alleged.

What wonder that the gods allowed numerous misfortunes to overtake mankind in an age so degenerate as to harbor these infamous folk in society. Tertullian had often heard base accusations leveled against Christians in Carthage. They were charged with causing all sorts of public disasters and national calamities. If the Tiber overran its banks, or the Nile unseasonably flooded the fields, or the heavens failed to yield rain, or earthquakes destroyed cities, or famine and pestilence were experienced in any quarter of the empire, the mob straightway shouted "Christians to the lion."[41]

[41] Tertullian, *Apology*, xl. 1 f. The popular charges against Christians have been elaborately assembled in the article, "Accusations contre les

Christians might reply, as Tertullian did, that the ignorant multitudes were deluded by demons and kept from worshiping the true God whom the Christians honored, and who, if revered by all men, would cure society of its ills. But the accusers were in no mood to hear defensive arguments from the victims of their hatred.

The practically minded official was as impatient as the mob with any explanations the Christians had to offer in defense of their position. Usually his hatred of them was not so extravagant as was that of the populace, and in fact he often wished to be lenient; but he could not endure stubborn disobedience, nor could he understand the conscientious scruples of the accused. To obey the command of the court was wise and virtuous conduct, while disobedience was ignorant folly or downright perversity. The magistrate might regret the stupidity of the recusants, but it was inexcusable and it necessitated immediate punishment. Respect for the sanctity of authority had to be maintained at any price.

The magistrate was, really, in a difficult position. Popular accusations had always played an important rôle in the administration of Roman justice.[42] They could not fail to affect the magistrate, even under emperors like Trajan, who definitely pronounced against giving heed to charges presented by anonymous in-

chrétiens," in F. Cabrol and H. Leclercq, *Dictionnaire d'archéologie chrétienne et de liturgie*, Vol. I (Paris, 1903), cols. 265-307.

[42] Note, for example, the remarks of Tacitus, *Annals*, IV. 36.

174

formers. And strong public opinion could never be ignored by those responsible for maintaining order. The rights of minorities could be given only secondary consideration by one anxious to acquire a good reputation as preserver of the peace in the opinion of the imperial master. Then, too, there were various well-attested phases of the Christian's social conduct that naturally aroused the suspicions of even the most fairminded Roman official.

As a matter of course Christians held meetings. This was inherent in the nature of the movement—a social necessity as well as a religious duty. The gentile church from its very inception had been essentially a social institution. While it is true that conversion to Christianity required a personal decision in response to a specific type of teaching, the process of Christianization was not accomplished until the convert became a duly constituted member of the new group, where he shared in its distinctive experiences, rites, and activities. For Christians to neglect the assembling of themselves together, either on account of the fear of the Roman authorities or because of an excessive stress upon the self-sufficiency of the individual, was a deplorable procedure.[43] Christianity was no mere philosophical movement, like the popular Stoicism of the day, where curious or serious individuals came together to hear the discourse of a teacher whose instruction could be personally appropriated and applied without involving one in the corporate life of a new society.

[43] Heb. 10:25.

175

Undoubtedly Christian leaders presented their religion to the Roman world as a new teaching—a new doctrine, dogma, philosophy. Paul was said to have procured at Ephesus the use of a lecture-room in the school of Tyrannus, where he expounded Christian teaching from eleven o'clock in the morning until four in the afternoon to anyone who cared to attend.[44] In the next century Justin at Rome carried on similar work in an upper room in Martin's house.[45] Pantænus in Alexandria set up virtually a Christian college which was continued by his more famous pupil and successor, Clement. Origen at Cæsarea and Lucian at Antioch carried on important Christian educational work. But these academic gatherings were not church meetings. They were, so to speak, only mission schools designed to interest and instruct individuals who might or might not belong to the church. The latter was the assembly of worshipers, the society of the initiated, corporate Christianity.

What went on in the meetings of the Christian assemblies? This was the question of chief concern to a Roman officer. He might discount the wild accusations of the mob, but he could not ignore the possibility that here he was face to face with a movement really deserving to be suppressed. If an emperor were suspicious of assemblies, on that ground alone his officers might feel in duty bound to prohibit Christian meet-

[44] Acts 19:9. The expression "from the fifth to the tenth hour" (i.e., 11 A.M. to 4 P.M.) is attested by ancient texts.
[45] Acts of Justin, III.

176

ings. These were religious gatherings where mysterious rites were performed, and this fact constituted, from the police point of view, a real danger. Even though much freedom was tacitly granted to many private cults in the imperial age,[46] it behooved a watchful official to be on his guard against Christian assemblies. If investigation showed them to be harmless, or if Christians temporarily ceased to hold meetings when the police intervened, they were still not necessarily innocent. Failure to worship the gods of the state and stubborn refusal to confess the lordship of Cæsar always seemed to make Christians potential, if not actual, enemies of the government.

Sometimes Christians themselves had been none too cautious in their efforts to placate the suspicious authorities. Instances of zeal to win a martyr's crown were at first occasionally in evidence, and magistrates were deliberately provoked to order executions that they would gladly have avoided. The wiser Christian leaders had to struggle against this frailty of their ardent brethren.[47] Yet the growing undercurrent of Christian hostility to the state was clearly apparent. As yet Christians who held office were few and Christian leaders disapproved of this form of activity for

[46] Cicero had said that all mystery ceremonies performed at night and participated in by women, with the exception of the ancient Demeter ceremonies, ought to be suppressed (*Laws*, II. 9). But under the Empire this rigid temper had greatly softened.

[47] Note the appeal of Ignatius to the Romans urging them not to use their influence to prevent his execution (*Rom.* i), and contrast the statement in the *Martyrdom of Polycarp* (iv), advising Christians against seeking to deliver themselves up to the authorities.

members of the church. If a soldier or a government employe accepted the new religion, an apologist might boast of the fact and tolerate his presence in the Christian society, but others were warned against seeking this type of occupation. Tertullian noted with some degree of pride that there were many Christians in the army, but he stoutly disapproved of the military profession. Christ had taken the sword away from Peter and had thereby unbuckled every soldier's belt. The purple, the fasces, and the rods—the insignia of authority among the Romans—had long ago been so defiled by their idolatrous associations that they could never be appropriately borne by a Christian. They were devilish paraphernalia, since "demons are this world's magistrates."[48]

Less belligerent critics were also stoutly opposed to a Christian's mingling in the affairs of state and they openly justified this continued aloofness. They supplemented their more distinctly Christian aversion by arguments that Stoics had been accustomed to use.[49] Christians declined public office because by so doing they could employ their time and energy in activities of greater value to society. So Origen reasoned. Not because Christians were hostile to the government, or were enemies of the state, but because they were occupied in serving God, it was necessary for them to refuse civic and imperial responsibilities; but by pursuing this policy they were in reality rendering to the

[48] Tertullian, *Idolatry,* xvii f.
[49] Cf. Epictetus, *Discourses,* III. 22. 8.

state the best possible service. Naturally, this point of view could not be appreciated by the Roman authorities. And the more influential Christianity became in society, the more menacing did it appear to be to the government. Slowly the political guardians came to realize that Christianity was gathering a social momentum that threatened to bring into being a new and essentially hostile state within the empire. Apparently Christians were not entirely unaware of their increasing power, as Origen made bold to intimate in his refutation of Celsus.

Origen could now look back upon a stretch of nearly forty years of almost unbroken peace in the relations between the church and the state. Philip the Arabian was emperor, and he was so favorably disposed toward Christianity as to give currency to the rumor that he had actually espoused this religion. Origen was not so optimistic that he failed to anticipate a further protest from the still powerful heathen party in the state, but he was convinced that Christians had now become sufficiently numerous and influential in society to lead a successful political revolution if God had seen fit so to decree. "Christians," he says, "because they were taught not to avenge themselves upon their enemies and have thus observed laws of a mild and philanthropic character, and because, although they were able, yet they would not have made war even had they received authority to do so,[50] have on this account re-

[50] Note the more rhetorical boast of Tertullian: "If we wished to play the part of open enemies, not merely the part of secret avengers, would

179

ceived it as a favor from God that he has always warred on their behalf and at times has restrained those who rose up against them and who wished to destroy them. For in order to remind others that seeing a few engaged in a struggle in behalf of religion they might also be better fitted to despise death, a few at various times, and these easily numbered, have endured death for the sake of the Christian faith; yet God did not permit extermination and destruction, since he desired that the Christian race endure and that its holy and blessed teaching should be spread throughout the whole earth."[51]

III

With the accession of Decius to the imperial authority, the relations between Christianity and the state entered upon a new stage. Previously Christians had not been systematically and persistently sought out in every locality by the authorities. But smoldering popular hatred might flame up into outbursts of violence

---

we lack in strength of numbers or resources? Are the Mauri and Marcomani and even the Parthians themselves, or any nation however great dwelling within its own boundaries, more numerous than one that is spread over all the world! . . . We would outnumber your armies, yes, we would be more numerous in a single province. For what war would we lack either the power or the courage, even if we were inferior in numbers, we who so voluntarily submit to death, were it not that according to our training we are required to submit to death rather than to kill" (*Apology*, xxxvii. 4 f.).

[51] Origen, *Celsus*, III. 8. Opinions vary as to the number of Christians who had actually been slain in the early persecutions. Accurate data are not available. Later legend reckoned them by millions, but a more sober historical criticism comes nearer to the views of Origen. See Linsenmayer, *op. cit.*, pages 48-52.

at any place and time. On these occasions the police and the magistrates felt entirely justified in resorting to extreme measures of suppression. But since the death of Marcus Aurelius (180 A.D.) only two relatively brief periods of persecution had been experienced by the church now rapidly growing in numbers and influence. Then came Decius with his deliberate attempt to uproot Christianity everywhere in the empire.

The motives that inspired the hostility of Decius, who in 250 A.D. issued his "deadly edict" as Christians called it, are readily understood. He was distinctly the Senate's emperor and represented the conservative tendencies of that body as they had not been espoused by any of his predecessors for upward of half a century. Consequently he set himself squarely against any policy of friendliness toward things Oriental, and the disposition to tolerate foreign religions. Toward Christianity in particular the Senate seems to have been hostile, an attitude which it retained long after the new religion had received the stamp of imperial approval under Constantine. Reviving the old Roman belief that the stability of the state depended upon maintaining the ancient religious rites, Decius zealously undertook their restoration.

One must not infer, as has sometimes been done, that Decius was motivated primarily by personal feelings of spite against his predecessor who had favored Christianity, or that his own hostility was simply the expression of an angry temper. The trouble was far more serious. The affairs of the state were in a precarious condition. Every day the menace of barbarian invasion was increasing, while the internal strength of the empire had been gradually crumbling. It was no time to disregard the ancestral gods under whose patronage Rome had been founded and ultimately raised to the status of world-dominion. The results of a thousand years of attainment were being endangered by neglect of the state's protecting divinities. Christians, whose numbers had rapidly multiplied in recent decades, were the chief offenders, and the health of the state seemed to require the complete suppression of this impious religion. The problem involved more than the exercise of mere personal likes or dislikes; the welfare of society and the safety of the government were the tremendous issues at stake.

Leading Christian thinkers had now adopted essentially the political philosophy of Rome. They agreed that the prosperity of the state could be insured only by the favor of heaven. But Christians added that they alone worshiped the Deity who was capable of maintaining the safety and prestige of the empire. As yet, however, they were not sufficiently numerous in society and influential in public affairs to convince an old-fashioned politician like Decius that the claim made for their God was valid. Yet Christians had become so conspicuous, and their disdain for the Roman deities was so outspoken, that Decius, not daring to entrust the destiny of his empire to Christianity's divinities, saw only one alternative. If the Christians were not, as they alleged, the best friends of the Roman

182

state, then they were its most dangerous enemies and their suppression was imperative.[52]

Decius, accordingly, undertook the task of obliterating Christianity from his domains. He aimed to crush the church as an institution and to force worship of the state gods upon all its members. It was not his purpose to effect a wholesale slaughter of Christians, and thus decimate the already declining population, but even that calamity was less to be dreaded than the presence in the empire of so many persons whose conduct glaringly offended the tutelary divinities. These "atheists" had to be eliminated at all costs. The instrument employed for accomplishing this result was an imperial edict, reinforced by specific instructions to governors and magistrates, sometimes aided by a local group of citizens. No one was to be allowed to escape notice. The new law had to be complied with by a fixed date, and provision was made for the issuance of certificates attesting obedience. No exception was to be made for dignity, sex, or age. Thus all Christians were to be reclaimed or suitably disciplined. This might be by death, or by forced labor in the mines, or by banishment. But capital punishment was resorted to only as an extremity. The emperor desired, rather, to force Christians to recant. If they refused they were horribly tortured and kept in wretched prisons where many of them slowly starved to death.

[52] Probably Cyprian (*Epistle* 55 (51). 9.) was right in saying that Decius would rather have seen a rival emperor set up against him than to have seen the appointment of a bishop of the Roman church to succeed Fabian, who had been executed early in the persecution.

183

While the Decian persecution was a severe blow to the church throughout the whole empire, it fell far short of demolishing the Christian religion. Even the church as a social institution survived, notwithstanding the deliberate policy of striking most immediately at its leaders and its economic resources. What the outcome would have been had Decius not met his death at the hands of the Goths less than two years after the promulgation of his edict of persecution, is a matter for speculation. But indications of failure were not lacking even before his death. A few prominent leaders of the church had perished, while others had successfully hidden until the peak of the storm had passed. Some Christians found refuge in flight to unknown parts, and many others discovered ways of evading the authorities without seriously disrupting their daily activities. Magistrates could be bribed, or other devices employed to cheat the Satanic persecutor and obtain the necessary certificate attesting conformity.[53] Great numbers of Christians no doubt outwardly complied by offering the sacrifices demanded and attending the feasts at the temple, but their obedience was only formal and the passing of the crisis found them back in the Christian gatherings. Their presence in the church now created a serious problem within its life, but even these "lapsed" Christians, as they

[53] On these certificates, the *libelli*, see J. R. Knipfing, "The Libelli of the Decian Persecutions," *Harvard Theological Review*, XVI (1923), 345-390; A. Bludau, *Die ägyptischen Libelli und die Christenverfolgung des Kaisers Decius* (Freiburg i. Br., 1931).

184

were termed had never been actually reintegrated within the heathen cults.

The successor of Decius, terrified by a pestilence that swept over the empire in the second year of his rule, temporarily renewed the attempt to make Christians worship the offended gods of the state. But the rulers were soon diverted by other troubles and the church enjoyed a five-year period of immunity. In the summer of 257 A.D. the Emperor Valerian resumed persecution. Again an effort was made to shatter the church as an institution by removing its leaders, depriving it of its properties, and treating with especial severity such of its members as belonged to the higher and more well-to-do classes of society. The first imperial edict ordered the discontinuance of all Christian meetings and the banishment of the clergy. The following year a second edict decreed the execution of the clergy, the degradation of all Christians of aristocratic rank, and the confiscation of their possessions. If these persons still refused worship to the old gods, the men were to be beheaded and the women banished. Christians found serving in the imperial palace, whatever their position might be, were degraded to the status of slaves and sent in chains to labor on the emperor's estates.

The legislation of Valerian, when compared with that of Decius, reveals a significant change in policy. The attempt to force the rank and file of Christendom to renounce their religion was not again undertaken. As an aggressive organized propaganda in society, drawing aristocratic people within the circle of its influence—members of senatorial and equestrian families —it was to be vigorously suppressed; but for those persons who might naturally adhere to a foreign cult Christianity did not seem an improper religion. The duty of these Christians to the state could be fulfilled by adding the worship of its greater gods to their patron deities.[54] But even this demand was not made with anything like the vigor that had been displayed by Decius. Undoubtedly Valerian had hoped that the breakdown of the church as an institution would permit, if not induce, the Christian populace to include worship of the official deities within the scope of their devotions without demanding that they "curse Christ."

The Roman officials may have learned two lessons from observing those who had "lapsed" in the Decian persecution. First, many of these persons had not really abandoned Christianity, even though they had sacrificed to Roman deities. And, secondly, if this procedure could be more amicably encouraged the formal respect for the state gods would be maintained without wrecking the social structure and sacrificing whatever measure of assistance any lesser divinities might be able to render the state. An old Roman like Valerian, who had been a censor, imbued with characteristic Roman ideas regarding the desirability of bringing all the divinities of all subjugated peoples into the service of the empire, could not be expected to appreciate the tenacity

---

[54] Observe the remark of the Prefect Æmilianus to Dionysius, bishop of Alexandria, reported in Eusebius, *History*, VII. 11. 9.

186

with which Christians feared the demons of idolatry and held to the notion of a jealous God.

Then, too, the calamities which the government had sought to avert by suppressing Christianity had multiplied rather than diminished, in spite of the heroic efforts of rulers to restore ancient religious rites. The pragmatic test of efficiency, even in matters of religion, always held an important place in the Roman administrative mind. Barbarian invaders were pressing in upon the empire all along the northern and eastern frontiers. Decius had been slain in battle with the Goths and Valerian was captured in his campaign against the Persians. The provinces had been ravaged by pestilences which had carried off half the population in some of the larger cities. Earthquakes, famine, drought, tornadoes and tidal waves had wrought great havoc. Industry and commerce had sadly declined, resulting in the impoverishment of the people, the depletion of the imperial resources, and the debasement of the coinage. After all, perhaps now, as in the period of the long-drawn-out conflict with Carthage, Rome needed some new increments of supernatural assistance.

So, perhaps, reasoned Gallienus, who succeeded Valerian in 260 A.D. At least he adopted the easier course of allowing freedom to all religions. With reference to Christianity he at once issued an edict restoring its confiscated properties and granting the right of assembly. Whether his action is to be understood as a formal edict of toleration legalizing Christianity in the Roman Empire, or only as a special measure permitting the church, particularly in Egypt, to hold property and assemblies, is uncertain.[55] In any event, Gallienus was never sufficiently powerful to enforce a law of universal toleration, as Decius and Valerian had, although with only partial success, been able to undertake a universal suppression; and the lack of a strong emperor during the following period of the "Thirty Tyrants" worked to the advantage of Christianity. For nearly half a century the church grew in power and social prestige, without serious interference from the authorities of the state.

The happy situation of the church was disturbed once more by the violent hostility of the political authorities under Diocletian. Undoubtedly he was one of the ablest emperors who had held office since Augustus, but he faced a Herculean task. The machinery of government had been almost completely wrecked by the preceding decades of anarchy and the successful aggressions of invaders. The political prestige of the empire had greatly declined and its economic resources were almost exhausted. Taxes were exorbitant, while poverty had increased and the cost of life's necessities had soared. It was a time of overwhelming depression.

[55] Eusebius, *History*, VII. 13, cites the communication sent by Gallienus to Dionysius and other Egyptian bishops: "I have decreed the beneficence of my gift to be distributed throughout all the world to the end that your places of worship shall be vacated (by the confiscators), and consequently you also can enjoy the privilege authorized in my rescript without anyone's molesting you. And this which you are permitted to do has already for a long time been granted by me. Therefore Aurelius Cyrenius, the chief minister of finance, will act in conformity with the rescript issued by me."

The spirit of national pride and patriotism seemed dead. The army had become a mercenary institution, composed mainly of barbarians, whose primary concern was their wages. The administration of government had passed almost completely into the hands of officials interested in personal gain and imperial favor. Loyalty to the state and devotion to the common welfare were virtues rarely to be found.

In the midst of the prevailing social chaos the church had become one of the most stable and influential institutions in the empire. It inculcated industry, frugality, and loyalty to a common interest, while the efficiency of its organization inspired confidence in its power. Not only the common man, who found asylum in the brotherhood, but persons of rank and culture discovered in Christianity a new focal point for the cultivation of their interests and the exercise of their energies. Thoughtful people, and even practical politicians, might well question whether hope for the empire did not really lie in the triumph of Christianity. But its increasing influence, from the point of view of outsiders, only accentuated the conviction that it was responsible for the troubles of the times. The more it grew the greater was the insult to the patron divinities of the state on whose favor the success of the empire was assumed to rest. Nevertheless, Diocletian, unlike Decius, did not initiate the task of rehabilitating the empire by persecuting Christianity. His vast work of reform had been under way for almost two decades before he attacked the Christian church. The marvel is that this action, which the logic of the situation rendered inevitable, should have been so long delayed.

In a world where an official state religion was universally believed necessary to the success of the political establishment, and where Christianity now occupied too conspicuous a position in society to be ignored, the authorities were forced to choose between three possible courses of procedure. An effort might be made to force the total personnel of Christendom to worship the official gods and utterly renounce their former faith. This attempt had been made by Decius. Or one might endeavor to break the power of the church as a religious organization, in the hope that Christians, left without leaders and institutional facilities, would return to the worship of the state gods, even if they perpetuated inconspicuously their disapproved private rites. This had been the policy of Valerian. A third possibility was to allow Christianity to exist among the multiplicity of cults ministering to the needs of the empire and adding to its resources of divine power whatever degree of potency each was able to contribute. This had been the plan of Gallienus, although it is doubtful whether he fully realized the distinctiveness of Christianity in holding that its God alone could save the state.

When Diocletian took deliberate action he followed the policy of Valerian. The specific motives that inspired Diocletian to promulgate a general persecution of Christianity in 303 A.D. are veiled in much obscurity, but the main factors in the situation are evident. It is easy to magnify his seeming friendliness toward Christianity, during the earlier part of his rule, as a foil against which to set off more glaringly the perversity of his later conduct. While he had not been an outright enemy of Christianity, and had been on friendly terms with prominent Christian persons, there is little to indicate that he ever regarded this religion as above suspicion or a desirable influence in his kingdom. He had never officially authorized a policy of toleration. Some of his closest associates in the government were Christianity's bitter foes, and hostile action by the authorities had occurred at different times throughout his reign. Wise ruler that he was, he hesitated to bring down upon his kingdom the devastation that would inevitably attend an effort to stamp out so powerful a religion as Christianity had become. But the religious psychology of Roman imperialism which he had thoroughly imbibed, as had his most efficient associates in the government, could not permanently endure a situation in which a powerful dissenting institution like the Christian church was allowed to prosper.

Diocletian's hostile action began with the destruction of the splendid Christian edifice in his capital, Nicomedia, on February 24, 303. This act was connected immediately with the celebration of the Roman feast of the Terminalia, by this date connected with Jupiter as protector of the boundaries of the empire. This conjunction of events was important, especially as Tiridates of Armenia, one of the trouble-makers on the eastern terminus of the empire, had accepted Chris-

191

tianity and legalized it in his domains. An edict was immediately promulgated ordering the destruction of all places of Christian worship, and the burning of all Christian books and other paraphernalia connected with worship. The aim was to crush the Christian cult and destroy the clergy, but to avoid, if possible, wholesale slaughter of individuals. Imprisonment, torture, and threats were employed to induce apprehended persons to sacrifice. Diocletian's retirement in 305 A.D. resulted once more in political chaos and left the rival claimants for power free to pursue their policies at individual will and to make such political capital as they could out of their attitude toward Christianity. In most instances they sided with heathenism against the Christian church.

IV

The history of these years is a cruel story that, fortunately, need not be rehearsed in the present connection. The fundamental issue remained unchanged. Was the right of the ancient divinities as the sole guardians of the state's welfare to be maintained, or was Christianity to be given a share in this task of guardianship? Even the stoutest persecutor, Galerius, who was now in control of the east, ultimately recognized the necessity of accepting the latter alternative. In the year 311 he issued an edict of toleration and posted it on the wall of the capital city, Nicomedia. Shortly afterward he died, and zealous Christian apologists from that day forward saw in his act only

192

the vain attempt of a frightened man to secure a death-bed forgiveness. Had he lived to put the provisions of his decree in force, Constantine might have been robbed of his doubtful glory as the first Christian emperor.

Galerius was no Christian, even on his death-bed. That fact is perfectly apparent from the language of his edict. Only by a reprehensible wresting of phrases from their context, and a generous use of imagination, can the traditional interpretation of this document be maintained. It simply recognized, in the practical hardheaded Roman way, the failure of persecution as a means of securing universal reverence for the deities of the state. It restored to Christians the right to worship in their own way, it admonished them to avoid agitating disturbances, and it appealed to them to pray to their God for the welfare of the ruler and the commonwealth, and the peace and prosperity of society.[56]

It remained for Constantine to pursue the new political policy to its logical conclusions.[57] The story of his

[56] The Latin version is contained in Lactantius, *Death of the Persecutors*, 34, and a Greek rendering is given by Eusebius, *History*, VIII. 17. 3-11.

[57] Much has been written about Constantine and his connection with Christianity. A more extended statement of the view presented here may be found in S. J. Case, "Acceptance of Christianity by the Roman Emperors," *Papers of the American Society of Church History*, second series, Vol. VIII (New York, 1928), pp. 43-64; and from a very similar point of view, N. H. Baynes, *Constantine the Great and the Christian Church* (London, 1931). Other books to note are E. Schwartz, *Kaiser Constantin und die christliche Kirche* (Leipzig, 1913); J. Maurice, *Constantin le Grand: L'origine de la civilisation chrétienne* (Paris, 1924); G. P. Baker, *Constantine the Great* (New York, 1930).

picturesque triumph over his foes in the west needs no retelling. Certainly he was convinced that the God of the Christians had supported his cause at the battle of Milvian Bridge. Henceforth he and his eastern colleague were determined to give the Christian Deity a responsible position in protecting their state. But they were not yet ready to trust everything to him. They were too thoroughly Roman to place the destiny of their kingdom in the keeping of any single divinity. They believed that the first duty of the princes was to set in order the rites of religion, without the proper observance of which no government could succeed. In order to accomplish this ideal they officially gave to the Christians "and to all men full freedom to pursue any religion that they chose, in order that whatever divine power there is in the celestial sphere may be favorable and propitious to us and to all those who are placed under our authority." Christianity was elevated to the full rights of a legal religion beside the older cults of the state. But lest Christians in their newly established liberty should override the proper bounds of toleration, the emperors were careful to reaffirm that the same liberty had been conceded to others also "in order that no dignity or worship may seem to be diminished by us."[58] This decision was reached early in February of the year 313.

Christianity had now won its struggle for political recognition; it had attained to the status of a legal

[58] The full document is contained in Lactantius, *Death of the Persecutors*, 48. 2 f.; Eusebius, *History*, X. 5. 2-14.

194

religion throughout the empire. Toleration was insured for all future time.[59] The eastern emperor, Licinius, who shared the rule with Constantine, had been less sympathetic toward Christians and showed some readiness to renew persecution. But his overthrow in 323 A.D. united the Roman world under a single ruler whose confidence in Christianity as the most competent religion to protect the state steadily increased. Under imperial patronage its prestige speedily mounted and the church rapidly consolidated into an institution whose power in society ultimately transcended even that of the imperial government itself.

It was in the very nature of ancient Christianity that it never could be content with mere toleration; its ideal could not be attained until it became supreme, first by supplanting all rival religions and ultimately by bringing even the political authorities under its domination. The first of these ambitions was more easily attained than the second. On the principle, universally accepted in the ancient world by both Christianity and the Roman government, that no state could prosper without an official religion, the rise of Christianity to a dominant position in society, in spite of the state's attempts at suppression, seemed unquestionably to demonstrate the superior efficiency of its divine resources. This conviction grew upon Constantine and his successors, who accordingly lent their aid to the

[59] Julian "the Apostate" (361-363 A.D.) favored heathen cults, but he did not institute a formal persecution of Christians. See W. D. Simpson, *Julian the Apostate* (Aberdeen, 1930).

195

growing church in its efforts to suppress not only rival religions, but also dissenting minorities within Christianity. An adequate official religion had to be not only supreme over all others, but a unit in its own operations. This practical interest prompted emperors, who favored or espoused Christianity, to take very seriously the controversies that raged within Christendom. Rarely had they any aptitude for following the intricacies of a theological argument or for judging as to the proprieties of an ecclesiastical practice. But they were tremendously concerned to preserve intact the integrity of the church as a social institution. Hence they always gave their support to that party which they believed to be the more powerful majority capable of perpetuating the established religion. The final decree of Theodosius, issued in the year 392, became the Magna Carta of orthodox Christianity's supremacy over all competitors in the religious arena.[60]

One more problem still awaited solution. There could not be two suns in the imperial sky. Did ultimate authority reside with the church or with the state? In Roman religion the state was always supreme. The will of the gods for human society was mediated by the authority of the Senate and the emperor, to whom all the priests or other functionaries of religion owed their existence and were responsible. In imperial times the ruler was the chief priest, *pontifex maximus,* a title retained by Christian emperors. It was inevitable

[60] The document is accessible in J. C. Ayer, *Source Book,* pp. 346 f.

196

that an institution entitled to exist within society by their decree should have been regarded as their servant. The state was superior to the church and the will of the Christian God, like the favor of the ancient Roman divinities, was insured to the state by the authority of the divinely approved ruler. Constantine, though desirous of receiving advice from the officials of the church as readily as heathen emperors sought guidance from their priests of religion, could never have tolerated for a moment any interference with his political activities from any Christian bishop.

In the earliest period of imperial favor Christians seem to have been content with this understanding of the relation between church and state. If Constantine sometimes failed in his personal piety and neglected to become a full-fledged member of the church, it was the duty of his Christian admirers to idealize his memory by lauding his virtues—which were many—and pointing to his acceptance of baptism the day before taking to his death-bed. He certainly had rendered the cause of Christianity a service which no amount of the most extravagant praise could adequately reward. Subsequent Christian emperors were not always so fortunate in satisfying the wishes of ecclesiastical leaders. Moreover, the church, not the state, was for Christians the supremely divine institution in society. Through its brotherhood, its sacraments, its worship, and the ministry of its clergy, help from God came to the devotees, whether they were the humblest of menials or the most dignified of aristocrats. Only through the medium of the church could the favor of Christianity's God be secured. It might now have been said of emperors, as it had been said of heretics in an earlier day, that "no one can have God for father who does not have the church for mother."[61] And only through the ministry of a properly authenticated priesthood could the efficacy of the divine institution be realized. From the ecclesiastical point of view the bishop was God's highest official among men, while according to the characteristically Roman way of thinking in imperial times this dignity resided in the political ruler. When the Christian God became the one divine protector of the state, was bishop or emperor supreme? The church had only one answer that could be given to this question. If imperialism were to survive as a political ideal, then it must be an ecclesiastical imperialism to which all political power would be subservient.

Christianity, having accepted the responsibility for furnishing to Roman society divine protection, a task which it had successfully declared the ancient deities incapable of performing, was now embarrassed by having on its hands two rival hierarchies, God's in the person of bishops and Rome's in the person of emperors. In the eastern part of the empire the power of the political prince maintained itself so successfully and supported Christianity so satisfactorily that ecclesiastical supremacy found slight opportunity or urge to develop a policy of aggressive self-assertion. But in the

[61] Cyprian, *Unity* 6.

198

west a different situation presented itself. Heathen religious survivals were still powerful, the Christian rulers of the state were often inefficient, the west had to bear the brunt of the barbarian invasion, and ecclesiastics were forced to assume the responsibility for both religious and political leadership. By virtue of circumstance Christianity in the western empire ultimately became an imperial institution charged with the task of administering or supervising all the affairs of state. There was no longer any area of political or religious activity over which the church did not exercise guardianship. Its social triumph was now complete.

V. *The Social Task of a Triumphant Church*

V

The Social Task of a Triumphant Church

CHRISTIANITY HAD AT LAST BEEN INTRUSTED WITH THE full guardianship of ancient society. How would it discharge this newly acquired responsibility? Its program of procedure was conditioned by both old and new forces. It possessed a complex heritage of customs and ideals that had been wrought out in the processes of real life during some three centuries of growth. On the basis of experiences thus acquired, Christian teachers were able to formulate a substantial body of social ideals. But these ideals could retain their validity only so long as the texture of the society that produced them remained essentially unaltered.

The centuries following Christianity's toleration by the Roman government witnessed changes quite as shocking to the stability of social life as anything that had been experienced in the course of Roman history during the previous period of the Christian movement's career. The battle line of social action presented a constantly changing front that rendered impossible any finished definition of the church's task. The social teachings expounded by Christian leaders at successive stages in the evolution of the religion's history were determined by changes in social practice that gradually emerged as the Christian way of life established itself in accordance with the necessities of existence experi-

203

enced by Christians as individuals and by the churches as groups in specific settings.

I

At the outset chief stress had been placed upon shaping the conduct of the individual, whose primary duty was to live pleasing to the Deity. The will of God had been discovered through contact with an individual teacher, like Jesus or Paul or other conspicuous preachers, whose message awakened the conscience of the hearer and sensitized the retina of his spiritual eye to perceive the divine in his own personal living. A rugged individualism demanded the realization of the highest type of character and the cherishing of the noblest aspirations of which the disciple was capable. This personal ideal remained a priceless heritage of the Christian cause for all time to come. Although he might never be able to fulfill his ambition, the Christian who aspired to attain to the highest degree of moral excellence envisaged a perfection in religious living such as he attributed to the very God whom he worshiped. And the church aimed to give to the world, in the person of its most worthy members, individuals who in all the contacts of life strove to exemplify the highest conceivable ideals of integrity, sincerity, unselfishness, and spiritual excellence.

In real life, however, Christians found themselves in a world of conditioning relations quite different from that in which their God and the angels in heaven dwelt. A church was no mere aggregate of socially

204

unrelated persons. Consciences and inner convictions differed with individuals; and the more sincere and earnest men were, the more serious was the clash of varying opinions likely to prove, so long as the individual standard remained supreme. But the group was a social entity, and the preservation of its integrity was early discovered to be essential to the continuation of the Christian movement. This discovery involved Christian teachers in a new task. They might try to unify the conduct and thinking of the group by demanding of every member conformity to older norms, but this was soon found to be an impracticable endeavor. If, for example, indifference toward worldly goods had once been the ideal type of conduct, a zealous preacher might state the traditional ideal in more emphatic form by demanding complete renunciation of possessions. But the effect of this procedure upon the perpetuity of the Christian group, now in need of more ample funds to support its enterprises and composed of persons earning a livelihood in various callings, would have been socially disastrous. A new ideal had to be created. Christian people were to be taught industry and frugality, and instructed in a Christian way of acquiring and using property for the good of the brotherhood. The needs of the society must transcend the whims of the individual.

The process of socialization exerted its formative influence over the whole range of the church's activities and teachings. There was no deliberate attempt to lower the ideals of the individual or to dull the voice of his conscience, but his conscience had to be educated in the sphere of larger social obligations and greater practical effectiveness for the welfare of the group. The situation presented the age-old problem of mollifying the ever-recurring struggle between the rights and duties of an aggressive individual as such, and the welfare and efficiency of the institution created by his predecessors to conserve and make effective the values bequeathed by them to the world. Ancient Christianity met this issue by attaching greater and greater importance to the perpetuation of the church as a social institution, whose integrity was safeguarded by a consistent repression of recalcitrant individualism —a procedure natural enough in the Roman world, although when judged by modern standards it may often seem to have been unwise if not excessively cruel.

The interpretation of the church's task in relation to its environing society underwent a similar development. At first Christian leaders had advocated a policy of aloofness. Social contacts in the civic community were to be eschewed, while the early Christian attitude toward the state had been one of respectful non-participation. In each of these areas of activity the actual social practice of Christians gradually nullified the ideals of the older Christian leaders and necessitated the formulation of a new type of social teaching. The church no longer took pride in pointing to the predominance of the lowly and uncultured in its personnel. Philosophers, men of high social standing, and

206

people of influence in governmental affairs were found to be too valuable to the success of the Christian cause to be avoided or despised. Ways of stating the Christian ideal of conduct in society had to be extensively revised to include many new spheres of activity lying far beyond the range of the earlier teachers' interests. And if Christianity was to maintain a desirable position of dictatorship over the morals of this more inclusive and diversified society, its teaching had to be of such a character as to be measurably practicable in the concrete situations of real life's varied complexities.

If the integrity of the Christian institution were to be preserved, it must now provide in its teaching for a variety of possibilities in the standards of living required of its members in different stations in life. A uniform rule could not be enforced; the church was no longer an assemblage of persons who had all attained to sainthood. One possible procedure would have been to lower all standards to the level of attainment thought possible of realization by the frailest member of the church. But this was not the solution adopted. Without abandoning its most rigorous ideals, Christianity made room within the institution for different grades of excellence in harmony with the capacity of its heterogeneous personnel. One who wished to detach himself as completely as possible from the life of the world might resort to a monastery and practice a rigid asceticism, while at the same time one whose life was inextricably entangled with mundane affairs was not forced to sever his connections with the church. This policy may easily be criticized as an unworthy compromise with the world, but it was tremendously significant for ancient society, in that it rendered possible an exercise of Christian influence over wide areas of life that would otherwise have been left without any healthful guidance.

By extensive readjustment—or liberal compromise, if one prefers to use the latter term—in the interpretation of its social task, the church was able to assume guardianship over widely diverse ranges of ancient life. Within the circle of the family, in the daily pursuits of the common laborer, in the market place and the forum, in the recreational activities of the community, in the administration of justice, in the cultivation of the arts, in the halls of learning, in the deliberations of the Senate, and even in the life of the imperial court, the voice of the church was heard insisting upon its supreme authority over all of society's concerns. If at first its mandates were unheeded, or only tardily obeyed, its injunctions might be prudently revised, but the note of authority in its utterances was never eliminated, and ultimately its will prevailed.

In assuming a comprehensive and detailed supervision over society's affairs, the ancient church had not acted in sheer presumption. In conformity with the mode of thinking prevalent in antiquity, Christian leaders assumed that social well-being was attainable only by means of Heaven's intervention in human concerns. The crucial task, therefore, was to provide for society an infallible agent through whom Deity could

208

operate on the mundane level. The church now believed itself to be, and was believed by its wards to be, the divinely appointed mediator of God's will for mankind. By the increase of its influence and power the city of God on earth, which was the ideal human society, had now become a concrete possibility. The church spoke by the authority of Heaven, whether it addressed the humblest man on the street or the highest potentate in the state. The very emperor who had legalized its claim to supremacy was forced to bow to its will, when Theodosius was refused the sacraments until he had performed the penance prescribed by Ambrose. An earthly ruler could ill afford to disobey a Christian bishop who had it in his power to determine the eternal destiny of an emperor's immortal soul.

The church had assumed a tremendous social obligation. In the name of Heaven it had accepted responsibility for rescuing the Roman Empire from all its troubles. The last obstacle in the way of carrying out this beneficent purpose had been removed when the political authority of the state placed itself at the disposal of the church. But this new implement had barely been acquired when the western empire "fell." Circumstance once again forced upon Christendom a reinterpretation of its social task.

The conviction that the church ought to be an imperial institution was too deeply ingrained to be completely dissipated even by the disruption of unified political power through incoming of the different barbarian peoples. But for the moment there was no single political authority capable of implementing the will of the church for the whole of society in western Europe. Temporarily, the social task of Christianity became more distinctly local and regional. Yet the church, now the most stable institution in every community, exerted a wide influence upon life. Barbarian princes, even though they might be Arians in theology, freely availed themselves of the help of the Catholic clergy in the administration of political and civic affairs. Often bishops were the most competent persons available to superintend the repairs of an aqueduct or to serve as advisers and agents of the government. And in the daily life of the citizen, the local church was the most substantial institution upon which he could depend to help him in the present and to insure the safety of his soul in the world beyond the grave.

It was a long while before the church consented to accept a state of affairs by which it was deprived of political authority to force its ideals upon society. Perhaps, indeed, even today the Roman church cannot heartily acquiesce in this limitation of its power. The efforts of the ancient church to restore imperial rule by the aid of Charlemagne and the establishment of the "Holy Roman Empire," and the heroic struggle of the mediæval papacy to maintain the supremacy of the imperially minded ecclesiastical institution over emperors and princes, are well-known facts of history. Back of them lay a religious motivation and a social philosophy inherited from the revered past, but not

210

always easy to understand in modern times. The program was out of harmony with the experience and temper of a new social order brought into being first by the rise of nationalism in Europe, and later by the rapid growth of the democratic temper in Europe and America.

Notwithstanding its loss of political authority, the Roman Catholic church still is keenly awake to social issues and maintains a well-defined social program.[1] In its interpretation, human values are still subordinated to divine concerns; and the church, as God's agent, is the only true guardian of society's well-being. In the last analysis worldly possessions are gifts of God, who created all things in the beginning and endowed men with power to develop a civilization and rear a social order for their profit and enjoyment. But this is not society's ultimate goal; the more important and comprehensive purpose of all human living is to prepare the soul for the eternal hereafter. Hence the primacy of the church in comparison with all other social institutions.

In all social evaluations, according to Roman Catholicism, the individual is the minimum limit, and God the maximum, on the same measuring scale. The highest good for the individual is what God wills, and

[1] Note the encyclical "Quadragesimo anno" on the "Restoration of the Social Order," issued by Pope Pius XI, May 15, 1931, in celebration of the fortieth anniversary of the encyclical of Leo XIII on "The Condition of the Workers." A very lucid interpretation of these two documents will be found in G. C. Rutten, *La doctrine sociale de l'église* (Liège, 1932) to which the official French translation of each encyclical has been appended.

highest good for society lies in the fulfillment by the individual of his personal duty according to his God-given capacity and opportunity. All problems of personal, professional, family, civic, national, and international duty are to be thus resolved; and the common good of society as a whole is the sum of all the good things in the material and moral sphere which men are able to procure for themselves in a well-organized society where each one serves the Deity according to the teachings of the church. This ideal is thought capable of safeguarding the weak, of restraining the strong, of insuring social justice in the economic and industrial sphere, of establishing harmony between rival peoples, and of making effective a universal peace under the guidance of the League of Nations. It is what Thomas Aquinas would call "the community of men under the mandate of God."[2] The realization of this ideal awaits only its voluntary acceptance by mankind—or the restoration of the church's imperial power to insure its enforcement.

The Protestant reformers interpreted the social task of the church entirely in the traditional manner. The ideal society was one whose procedures were ordered according to the will of God, which could not be truly known outside of the Christian group. As an institution the church constituted an ideal society, charged with the responsibility of supervising the total conduct of its members over the whole range of their social contacts. The ultimate duty of the church was

[2] *Summa* I. ii. Quest. 100, Art. 5.

to prepare souls for heaven. As God's instrument dedicated to this high service, it stood ready, when circumstances permitted, to enforce its regulations over the whole range of society's operations. In this respect Protestantism differed from Roman Catholicism at only one vital point. That was the question of the specific means by which God's will for society could be known. According to Protestantism, it was to be sought in the divinely inspired Scriptures, while Catholicism derived it immediately from the divinely authenticated ecclesiastical institution.

Although Protestant Christianity had at the start assumed responsibility for the comprehensive direction of such units of the social order as came within its reach, it presently found its control rapidly weakening over wide areas of men's interests and activities. Radical changes in the social structure within those territories where the Protestant churches have been the strongest from the sixteenth century to the present time have rendered quite obsolete Protestantism's original conception of its social task. The details of those changes constitute too long and intricate a story to be traced in the present connection.[3] But the outcome is familiar and its results spell despair for one who endeavors to define the social task of the church at the present time. Protestantism today presents no unified and generally accepted body of opinion on

[3] This story may be pursued in an already extensive literature. See, for example, R. H. Tawney, *Religion and the Rise of Capitalism* (New York, 1926); E. Troeltsch, *Sociallehren* (cited above, p. 47); and the works referred to by these writers.

what the church ought to undertake in the sphere of social action, or what means can be effectively employed to make Christianity a dominating influence in modern society.

An attempted solution of all the grave issues presented by the modern situation would necessitate an unwarranted digression from the main theme of the present study. But one question seems appropriate. Does the triumph of the church in ancient society shed any ray of light upon the social task of present-day Christianity?

II

A word of caution at this point may not be out of place. It would be quite unfair to the Christianity of ancient times to measure the worth of its social attainments by the demands of modern conditions or to assume that a social program, formulated to meet situations in the Roman world, must justify itself by demonstrating its efficiency to solve present-day problems. An assumption of this sort is liable to a double error.

In the first place, one may be led to imagine that ancient Christianity must be made to authorize every social ideal and activity proper for the church in the world of today. This has been a widely current inference within both Catholicism and Protestantism. The loyalty of the former to its divinely established institution, and of the latter to its divinely inspired Scriptures, gave to both communions an authoritarian cast

214

of thought that could not be easily transcended when the church was called upon to deal with new social problems. Catholic leaders turned for instruction to the papacy, while Protestants sought guidance from a fresh concatenation of biblical texts. The Christianity of the past furnished legislation rather than inspiration for the solution of modern issues.

Protestants of the so-called "liberal" school have endeavored to simplify their task by reducing the Scriptural norm to words spoken by Jesus. From him one seeks the authoritative message of a social gospel for a modern age. His challenging summons to love one's neighbor as one's self, and to practice in all the relations of life a purity of motive and a spirit of devotion to truth and goodness in no respect inferior to the standards of God himself, is as worthy a text as any Christian preacher could possibly desire. But the detailed application of this text to modern social conditions causes the preacher much perplexity, if it does not indeed drive him to despair. He can only infer, in the light of his own best judgment, how Jesus would have proceeded had he faced the concrete situations of the present hour and consented to set himself up as a judge and divider in a modern dispute between the capitalist and the laborer, or in a conflict between rival nations each obsessed by the conviction that its cause is just.

The social task of the church today is in serious danger of being distorted, and our vision thrown out of focus, by a false notion that the ancient church, or

215

even Jesus himself, delivered final legislation with reference to our immediate situation. Our perspective needs to be corrected by remembering that most of the baffling social problems of today were quite unknown to the ancients. The early Christians dwelt in a world bounded by the frontiers of the Roman Empire and peopled by races whose social experience had been measurably unified by close intercourse within relatively narrow geographical and temporal limits. The structure of Roman society was not lacking in complexities, but it was marvelously simple in comparison with that of the modern world.

Modern social distress is staged on a world-scale. Its manifestations reach around the globe, and no facilities seem to have been provided for ringing down the curtain on the final scene. Jesus, on the other hand, lived within the narrow confines of Palestine, where his observations were restricted within a few hundred square miles of territory occupied by a population that can hardly have exceeded a million inhabitants. The earth then was not served by controlled electric currents momentarily spreading news of the world's doings over radio, telephone, telegraph, and cables encircling the globe. Ocean liners and transcontinental railways had not blended into one social whole the peoples and the commerce of all nations. No daily newspapers flaunted the doings of all mankind into the face of Jesus and his disciples while they ate their morning meal. They were not compelled, nor would they have been able had they so desired, to live amid

216

the complexities of our intricate social order. It is unfair to demand that they should diagnose unknown maladies and prescribe remedies for non-existent diseases.

If Jesus and the early Christian missionaries were upon earth today preaching in the interests of the kingdom of God, how vastly more complex would be the task they must visualize! In respect to space alone a tremendous readjustment of perspective would be necessary. Preaching to "all the nations" would carry them far beyond the River Indus on the east and the Pillars of Hercules on the west. The ideal assemblage of representatives from all peoples of the earth, who heard the gospel in their several tongues on the first Christian Pentecost, would have to be extensively supplemented. Of the lands and peoples comprising the world today, only a minor portion is embraced in "Parthians and Medes and Elamites, and the residents in Mesopotamia, in Judea and Cappadocia, in Pontus and the Province of Asia, in Phrygia and Pamphylia, in Egypt and the regions of Libya about Cyrene, and visitors from Rome, both Jews and proselytes, Cretans and Arabians."[4] Vast areas of the earth's surface utterly unknown to the first Christians, and races and cultures of whose existence they had never dreamed, have now become vitally involved in the still unsolved problem of establishing the kingdom of God among men. Today the realization of this ideal demands a globe-encircling program embracing all races and

[4] Acts 2:9-11.

217

classes of society throughout the five continents and on thousands of islands dispersed over the seven seas.

The notion of time, too, has been tremendously elongated. The society to be redeemed by the Christian preacher today has been in the making for long millenniums. He can no longer assume, in Pauline fashion, that his task can be accomplished by eliminating from human nature an Adamic taint injected into society by demonic action shortly after the year 4004 B.C. Rather, he must battle with evil impulses that have been bred in the blood of the human brute since perhaps the days of the Neanderthal man. The accumulated momentum of evils today embodies forces inherent in human nature since the dawn of civilization and fortified by habits of selfishness and greed that have been intrenching themselves in society for possibly half a million years. To bind the "strong man" of wickedness and plunder his domains becomes a far more formidable undertaking when it is seen to demand a tedious transformation of age-old human natures than could have been imagined when it was supposed to involve simply the ejection of some temporary Satanic interloper in the affairs of mankind.

Similarly, the range of one's gaze into the future has been vastly lengthened since the days when the first Christians began their heroic struggle to make righteousness triumphant upon earth. Their ardent faith in the ultimate victory of God over Satan, with all that it would mean for humanity, is beyond question the grandest social vision that has ever been conceived. But the inspiration of that vision grows dim and its driving force is sadly impaired if unreleased from the temporal categories of ancient thinking. The earliest Christians believed that only a brief stretch of time had been allotted to them for performing their part in bringing about the new social order. They were to prepare the way for God's speedy intervention. Their successors had to learn new lessons in endurance and to assume a larger measure of responsibility, as they perceived that the time had not been shortened, but had been greatly lengthened, in order that Christianity might have ample opportunity to demonstrate its value to mankind on the continuing mundane level. We ought not to demand that ancient Christians furnish us a rule for measuring the time within which Christianity's social mission is to be completed. They were unable to view the task from the perspective of the length of days that stretches out before the eye of the twentieth-century man.

There is a wide range of social tasks characteristic of today's needs that were but dimly, if at all, perceived in ancient times. However loyal the individual may wish to be to his Christian heritage, he frequently finds it deficient as a guide for his conduct when he is faced by some of the most crucial issues of the present. Even the problems of personal conduct have taken on many new aspects in the history of social evolution since the time of Jesus. The Christian is well aware that he should be peace-loving in his relations with other members of the community, yet there are times

219

when he feels it absolutely necessary to appeal to the coercive power of law to secure a just procedure that could never be obtained by holding literally to early Christian teaching about not resisting evil. Hostile forces in the present environment have become too intricate and powerful to be controlled effectively without resort to law courts and police, or other means of physical self-protection. These safeguards are so integral a part of our social well-being that a religious person is compelled to assume a positive and constructive attitude toward activities that might once have seemed entirely secular and beyond the range of his serious concern.

One living in Palestine at the beginning of the Christian Era might have felt quite justified in taking an attitude of indifference or aloofness toward a civil state presently to be supplanted by a new order inaugurated by the direct action of Deity. Temporarily, the things that are Cæsar's and the things that are God's could be sharply distinguished, and Cæsar could be tolerated until God had set up his triumphant regime. But our situation involves us directly in the physical paraphernalia of a society within which God seems to have commissioned us to set up his better kingdom by giving more diligent heed to the things that once were thought to be peculiarly Cæsar's. Our obligations as members of modern society require that we shall vote for this or that candidate for office, support one or another political platform, and take a positive stand on all proposed legislation affecting the well-being of ourselves and our fellows.

This concern with the technique of the civic order, although quite foreign to early Christian ways of thinking, has become absolutely essential to an effective Christian social program under twentieth-century conditions. In the setting where Jesus and his companions lived there was no occasion for a religious teacher to busy himself with educating people to discharge the duties of democratic government. It had not dawned upon the world in those days that responsibility for producing an honest and competent administration of civic and national affairs rested ultimately with the voter who cast his ballot at an election. By force of circumstances the ancient church was relieved of the duty or the opportunity of framing specific rules for the guidance of religious individuals or groups in a democratically organized society.

Christianity has long maintained that "man shall not live by bread alone." Yet no physical organism can permanently survive without food. A mundane kingdom of God will certainly insure for mankind a suitable share of the world's material goods. In the Roman Empire where Christianity arose there were poor, homeless, ill-clad and hungry people in abundance. But in comparison with the hordes of needy humanity known to us today, the indigent elements in the population of Palestine in the time of Jesus, or even the needy to whom the early gentile missionaries preached, sink into relative insignificance. China's starving millions, robbed of food by recurrent droughts and floods and wars, needy thousands in the overcrowded areas of Japan, and vast numbers of people all over the world at present who are denied the opportunity to earn a livelihood under existing conditions of depression, present an almost incomprehensible picture of actual and potential suffering made all the more acute by the vision of the higher standards of living set up by a modern civilization. Its like the world has never before consciously witnessed. Certainly no early Christian was in a position to visualize the enormities and cruel contrasts exhibited in the modern economic crisis.

The difficulties for the Christian church today are further enhanced by the fact that men go hungry, unclothed, unhoused, and suffer other physical privations, in a world where the material resources for meeting their needs exist in abundance. The farmer is impoverished, not because his fields are barren, but because he cannot dispose of his surplus products. The landlord in the city is unable to pay his taxes, not because he has no apartments, but because he has no paying tenants. The manufacturer goes bankrupt while his warehouses are bursting with unsold commodities. And producers of various sorts of goods needed by society are helpless through inability to market their wares. At the same time, multitudes of would-be consumers, physically competent and willing to work, are suffering because they have not the means with which to purchase life's bare necessities. This is a distressing state of affairs resulting from an economic order whose complications and genius were quite unknown in ancient times.

In accordance with what pattern the multiple threads in our intricate economic life ought to be interwoven, is one of the most perplexing issues confronting modern religious leaders who would frame a social program for the church. Early Christians knew practically nothing of the peculiar difficulties involved in the present situation. Adopting the gospel injunction, one might say to a property-holder, "Go sell all you have and give to the poor." But at present no one will buy. And in the event that a purchaser were found, what advice should be given to the new holder of the property? It is likewise futile, under present-day conditions, to admonish the poor man to take no thought for the morrow, but to live care-free like the birds of the air. He knows too well the disastrous consequences sure to follow this type of conduct under existing social conditions. Certainly Jesus and his disciples, when speaking on economic issues, were not concerned with the actualities of a modern capitalistic society. Whether this society be regarded as good or bad, it is a new thing that has appeared in the world long since Christianity arose, and its problems cannot be solved by the application of any ancient rule. While the early church met poverty with a magnificent charity, it offered no program for the reconstitution of the social order to insure the elimination of poverty, and an equitable distribution of the world's goods to everyone willing to bear his share in the task of production.

223

Still another, and perhaps the most formidable, modern social evil, is the menace of international conflict. Warfare has long been a curse to society and its devastations were all too well known to people in the Roman Empire. Yet in comparison with the colossal destruction of life and property wrought by war in this enlightened twentieth century, Roman military activities were mere police skirmishes and belonged, as it were, on the periphery of society. Soldiering was then an occupation in which men engaged for hire; it did not demand the life blood of the empire's youth in the name of patriotism. A phenomenon like the late World War was unknown and unimaginable in early Christian times. Never before have so many peoples of the earth been drawn into the whirlpool of conflict or affected so widely by the debilitating consequences that have followed this riotous holiday in honor of Mars. The like has never before been experienced by mankind on so wide and far-reaching a scale. And to add to the confusion of the church, those peoples and nations most active in the conflict have for centuries professed at least nominal allegiance to the Prince of Peace.

It is no easy task for the Christian church to plot its course of action in relation to the national and international issues that have grown out of the World War. Would that the ancient church had spoken some authoritative word for our guidance! While the conflict was raging sincere Christians on both sides of the battle line with equal fervor besought God for victory.

Participation in the deadly strife as a Christian duty was preached from thousands of pulpits in both hemispheres; piety and patriotism became synonymous terms. Like Augustine in the early fifth century, Christian prophets in the twentieth century justified participation in a war to end war; they would fight to win a glorious victory for eternal peace. But has this ideal goal been attained by anyone except the millions who lie buried in the graves of the slain?

Society is still left with the task of eliminating warfare. It is one of the most crucial problems confronting the church today, and far too complex to be solved by the simple injunction to turn the other cheek. One may place great hopes in a League of Nations, a Kellogg Peace Pact, an Institute of Pacific Relations, and international conferences on the limitation of armaments and the readjustment of reparations, or other efforts to establish comity and understanding among men of different races and nations. But as yet these are only faint whispers scarcely heard above the din of voices clamoring for the maintenance of armaments, aggravating national jealousies, and demanding the erection of tariff walls and the rearing of immigration barriers to secure special privileges for national or racial groups. In all of these matters the church is still rather blindly feeling its way. What will be its answer when it is asked whether there can be a Christian patriot, and, if so, what should be his attitude when his country's safety seems menaced by a rival nation, particularly if its citizens are also adherents of the Christian religion? Ancient Christianity offers no detailed solution for the perplexing issues involved. This is a situation that was never confronted by Jesus and his disciples.

III

Granting that the world today presents a wide range of issues unknown to the early Christians, shall we conclude that the triumph of the church in ancient society has no meaning for religion in modern times? This is a second error to which we are liable.

Within the circles of present-day Protestantism the determination of Christianity's proper social task, and the formulation of an approved program for action, have been attended by many difficulties. For perhaps half a century there has been an ever-increasing conviction among Protestant leaders, sensitive to the injustices and evils in modern life, that the present structure of society ought to be more thoroughly Christianized. To effect this end the most obvious course of procedure at first seemed to be to gather up from the Christian past, particularly from the teaching and attitudes of Jesus, rules for conduct that would, if obeyed, resolve the difficulties. One sought to make known the supposed will of Jesus with reference to relieving the unhappy conditions of large elements in our population who had been caught in the meshes of an increasingly perplexing social process. It would be difficult to estimate in full the benefits that have resulted from the prophetic zeal with which this stirring social gos-

226

pel has been preached by men of vision and consecration, like the late Professor Walter Rauschenbusch, whose memory is honored in this annual series of lectures. But the tardiness with which the leaven of this new social vision has permeated modern life has, to say the least, had a very sobering influence upon our optimism.

The challenging task of Christianizing society remains as yet largely unfulfilled. If discouragement looms menacingly upon our horizon, a measure of consolation may be derived from remembering how long were the years of struggle necessary to the triumph of ancient Christianity within Roman society. The victory was not attained in one generation, or in a single century; and when triumph came the result involved many readjustments in plans and ideals to meet new conditions of life that an ever-changing social environment imposed upon the success of the Christian movement. Social teaching had to be recast from time to time in accordance with the necessities of social living. Thus ancient Christianity triumphed as a way of life, and so phrased its gospel that it could be practiced by people who were willing to strive toward standards that were not wholly out of reach and surmount barriers that were not utterly beyond their capacities. Measured by the highest conceivable ideals, the progress registered at any particular stage in the development may seem to have been relatively meager; but, viewed from the point of departure of the individuals and the groups engaged in the actual task of

227

living the Christian life in widening social contacts, the accumulated result of some three centuries of effort rendered Christianity triumphant. The social attainments of the ancient church are, of course, not the specific goals to be aimed at by religion in modern society. In the meantime the world has tremendously changed, and with new conditions the social obligations of Christianity have correspondingly altered. But the nature of the struggle remains essentially the same. If the church is to win a social victory in the modern world, Christianity must make itself a practicable religion for people who participate in the complex activities of the social process. It is only they who can create a Christianized social order.

Two goals, adopted successively, were envisaged by the early church. The first was the winning of individual converts who, as a Christian group, would constitute a new social unit within an irredeemable environment that ultimately would be abolished by a sudden act of God. Thus the whole social order would finally be Christianized by the future intervention of divine power from without. As the doctrine of a catastrophic end of the present world was pushed into the more distant future, a second goal was adopted. The new aim was to bring the entire social order of the Roman world under the power of the Christian ecclesiastical institution. This end had been virtually realized by the ancient church in the early fifth century.

A third type of effort, more distinctly characteristic of the modern situation, was not deliberately undertaken by the ancient church. That is the problem of making the Christian ideas of justice, brotherhood and spiritual idealism prevail in a society whose structure, techniques and operations are not to be brought under direct ecclesiastical control. The state church of antiquity gave its blessing to the organized mechanisms of Roman society, without proposing any extensive reorganization of the social machinery, beyond the requirement that its administrators should be held amenable to the ecclesiastical authorities. Today, from the Protestant point of view at least, two revisions in the ancient procedure seem inevitable. The church does not wish to assume official responsibility for the management of the world's economic, political, and cultural affairs; nor does it agree that the techniques employed by modern society in these areas of human interest are necessarily entitled to Christian approval. Does not this attitude leave the modern church in an impossible position? This difficulty is central in any effort to define the social task of Protestant Christianity today.

The American dogma of strict separation between church and state seems to have borne both sweet and bitter fruit. It insured for the individual the blessed privilege of freedom to follow unhindered the dictates of his conscience in religious affairs. Not only coercion by the state, but forcible restraint on the part of any religious group to which he might originally have belonged, was completely eliminated. If he found conditions uncongenial in a particular church he separated himself from its fellowship, and if he could gather a like-minded few ready to join with him, a new denomination arose and acquired legal status simply on its own request. Thus Protestant bodies multiplied profusely, until the social integrity of Protestant Christianity as a whole, and the sense of Christian responsibility for the operations of so-called secular affairs, almost reached the vanishing point. Under these circumstances the recovery of a lively social consciousness on the part of such Christian people has been exceedingly difficult. As yet they have been unable to unify the operations of even their own ecclesiastical groups, and have been correspondingly ineffective in bringing their religious ideals to bear upon the activities of society at large.

American Protestantism has thus become exceedingly individualistic in its conception of religion; and its social consciousness, which has been extensively aroused in recent decades, still seeks release in strongly individualistic ways. The religious teacher's first concern is to exalt worthy ideals of personal conduct in all the relations of life, and to persuade members of the church in their various social contacts to emulate these ideals. The evils of society are attacked in a similar way. The blame for social ills is placed primarily upon persons who take advantage of opportunities for exploitation that an inadequately organized social structure makes possible. Religion's task is to inspire righteous conduct and to denounce the offenses of sinners, in the hope that the result will lead to an improved social order. There can be no reasonable doubt about the primary importance of religion's insisting upon the highest conceivable ideals of personal righteousness. This task ought to be performed with ever increasing diligence, but is there not a further work to be undertaken by the church?

Every student of social processes knows that the temper and conduct of a group tends to fall below the moral standards by which members of the group as individuals usually seek to regulate their personal lives. People who would not tolerate for a moment the possibility of murdering one of their neighbors, even though he were an irritating business rival, will, under the influence of the group spirit of patriotism, enthusiastically indorse wholesale murder in warfare. Political, commercial, and industrial groups practice moral codes that permit operations of graft, greed, and violence quite out of accord with the private habits of persons who compose the group. There is one standard for the individual and another for the herd. Even members of the church, when engaged in secular activities, have often assumed that their personal character is not involved with the moral quality of action by the secular group to which they belong. In an age that deliberately countenances the self-determination and independent development of secular society, the task of religion in attempting to improve the moral quality of group action is exceedingly perplexing.

The church today is faced by the problem of implementing its social ideals for the welfare of all mankind. It no longer confines its attention to the immediate task of encouraging good living among individuals within the ecclesiastical groups; it perceives that the warp and woof of the social web are so intricately blended that the moth and rust of moral turpitude affecting any part of the fabric are a menace to the well-being of the whole. We must return to the ancient church's task of bringing the entire social order under the influence of the Christian ideal, even though we may have to rephrase the ideal and devise a new program for the accomplishment of our purpose. As in times past, so today, a socially aggressive Christianity must expect to meet with strong opposition from forces that resent or dread its interference. The critic will remind us that it is the business of the church to deal exclusively with spiritual affairs and not to degrade religion by dragging it down to the secular level —as though conditions under which men earn a livelihood and maintain their daily existence in a complex social organism had nothing to do with their spiritual health.

In Protestant America the dogma of separation between church and state has generally been so interpreted—or rather misinterpreted—as to deny the Christian minister the right to discuss questions of human welfare and social justice in his pulpit, or to participate in social activities to improve the moral quality of the community's daily living. If he attacks perverse operations in business or politics he is sure to be charged with ignorance and is informed that he is meddling in that which is none of his business. Pernicious vested interests will declare him to be a menace to the public welfare, if not indeed an unpatriotic citizen. But such criticisms, unpleasant as they may be, are manifestly too selfish and unsound to block permanently the way toward that larger Christian activity beckoning the church forward in these days of crying social need.

Of course it is not impossible that we ministers may talk unwisely and propose foolish panaceas in moments of high emotional tension when stung by the sight of some monstrous social evil in our community. Perhaps our theological seminaries of the last generation trained us more diligently in the principles of biblical hermeneutics than in the fundamentals of modern social living. We are justly discounted if we play the rôle of amateur social theorists. But we may count on being heard with gladness, even by those who are bearing the heaviest responsibilities in society, if we show ourselves aware of the serious difficulties involved in the operations of the social mechanism and are keenly sensitive to the selfishness and dishonesty in public life that masquerade under the cloak of superior business acumen and political sagacity.

The Christian minister is the herald of righteousness, not alone for the individual church member, or for the ecclesiastical group, but for the community, the nation, and the world at large. This is the comprehensive task of the Christian church today. But what techniques it shall employ for making effective a higher social righteousness is the baffling problem. There are those who pronounce religion bankrupt at this point. The tardiness of the church in awaking to this task, and the exaggerated individualism of Protestant attitudes during the last half century or more, have led some persons to believe that social regeneration must proceed without benefit of clergy or church. Secular agencies alone are said to be adequate to the task.

The Christian church today is a vast social institution, though temporarily shorn of much of its native strength by disunion and inertia. Sometimes we are told that it is incapable of recovering its power, and that we can hope for social justice only as depressed groups seize secular authority and thereby overthrow rival empowered groups.[5] There is much food for serious thought in this proposition. Advances in social evolution have too often seemed impossible except through resort to violence. And who can say that in this respect history will not repeat itself! But this eventuality would not solve the fundamental social problem for the human race as a whole. To pass power and special privilege from one group to another—say from the capitalistic to the laboring class—might be only a transference of allegiance from the god of mammon to the god of brickbats. We should still be left with the task of establishing the supremacy of rational, moral, and spiritual interests within the new regime.

The Christian church is not so helpless, or the sig-

[5] This is the thesis, for example, of R. Niebuhr, *The Contribution of Religion to Social Work* (New York, 1932), developed at greater length in his *Moral Man and Immoral Society* (New York, 1932).

234

nificance of its activities so futile, as in our impatience we may have sometimes assumed. As a social institution its influence has been great in the past, and is still not without power. Its movements at times may seem lumbering and uncertain; it does not flash to its goal with meteoric brilliancy. But it is busy planting the grain of mustard seed—the demand for brotherhood, justice, honesty, peace and righteousness—not only in individual lives, but in the social order. It hesitates again to seek political authority with which to implement its social ideals; but its organized efforts are not without effect upon people in authority. Politicians know too well the power of a delegation of Christian clergymen to refuse them an audience when they bear to the Prime Minister of England their protest against the multiplication of armaments. And the voice in America of the Roman Catholics, and of the Federal Council of Protestant Churches, raised against economic injustice, are further significant signs of the times.

The church no longer enters as a competitor in the political arena, but it is an increasingly powerful factor in the shaping of public opinion, and its influence will enlarge as it emphasizes, and participates more extensively in, social action. Our road to accomplishment lies along the highway of practical activities. This was the secret of the early church's triumph, and it is the line of procedure that promises the church a new success in the modern world. The ministers of religion will, it is to be hoped, continue to proclaim the highest

235

social ideals that they can derive from the past or discover in their own immediate experiences; yet they must not lose sight of earth while their vision ranges to the skies. The otherworldly life has its attractions and its peculiar glory, but social ills today demand for their healing a technique and a program thoroughly informed by the possibilities of success within a situation where full account is taken of the limitations of human beings and the realities of our actual world.

The task of the church cannot be adequately discharged simply by announcing what an ideal kingdom of God should be, and then leaving society to marvel at—or forget—the picture. It would be a sad day if the Christian ministry lost its prophetic message of warning, but it will be sadder, perhaps, if it fails to work its healing art effectively upon a sick society. We must protest against the low moral standards sometimes displayed in our national and international politics, in the greed of our competitive commercialism, or in the maladjustments of our industrial world. But to preach a message that calls for the complete elimination of these evils in the world today, before our social gospel can begin its constructive operations, will hardly produce the Utopia for which we yearn. Like the early church, we too must strive to accomplish the possible while we are hoping for the attainment of the impossible. We must learn to say "one step enough for me," as we seek to help men today to advance gradually toward a more satisfactory status of human relations in our present world.

236

If Christianity is to succeed as a social restorative it must be made a way of life possible for men under existing circumstances. Instead of holding aloof from various forms of activity that in these days have often been called purely secular, Christians might well seek, as Christians, full participation in such activities. Let the church not hesitate to undertake the solution of international, national, civic, economic, and industrial problems—and let it not be too sure that it has a ready-made program for resolving every difficulty that may arise. Its task is to evolve practical ways of helpful procedure on the basis of accumulated experience and in the light of actual conditions. As in the history of the early church, so today success can come only through a long process of social effort as the church leads and shares in the concrete task of helping people live together in a real world. The most effective way to Christianize the social order is to socialize the Christian religion.

THE END

Index

239

INDEX

243

INDEX

244

INDEX

245

INDEX

246

INDEX

INDEX

INDEX

250

479